FIVE ENGLISH REFORMERS

J. C. RYLE

THE BANNER OF TRUTH TRUST

THE BANNER OF TRUTH TRUST
3 Murrayfield Road, Edinburgh EH12 6EL
PO Box 621, Carlisle, Pennsylvania 17013, USA

*

First published in *Light from Old Times* in 1890
Five English Reformers first published in 1960
Second impression in 1961
Third impression 1965
Revised edition 1981
Reprinted 1994
Reprinted 1999
ISBN 0 85151 138 4

*

Printed in Finland by
WSOY

CONTENTS

WHY WERE OUR REFORMERS BURNED?

There are certain facts in history which the world tries hard to forget and ignore. These facts get in the way of some of the world's favourite theories, and are highly inconvenient. The consequence is that the world shuts its eyes against them. They are either cut dead as vulgar intruders, or passed by as tiresome bores. Little by little they sink out of sight of the students of history, like ships in a distant horizon, or are left behind like a luggage train in a siding. Of such facts the subject of this paper is a vivid example: "The Burning of our English Reformers; and the Reason why they were Burned."

It is fashionable in some quarters to deny that there is any such thing as certainty about religious truth, or any opinions for which it is worth while to be burned. Yet, 300 years ago, there were men who were certain they had found out truth, and were content to die for their opinions. It is fashionable in other quarters to leave out all the unpleasant things in history, and to paint everything with a rose-coloured hue. A very popular history of our English Queens hardly mentions the martyrdoms of Queen Mary's days! Yet Mary was not called "Bloody Mary" without reason, and scores of Protestants were burned in her reign. Last, but not least, it is thought very bad taste in many quarters to say anything which throws discredit on the Church of Rome. Yet it is as certain that the Romish Church burned our English Reformers as it is that William the Conqueror won the Battle of Hastings. These difficulties meet me face to face as I walk up to the subject which I wish to unfold in this paper. I know their magnitude, and I cannot evade them. I only ask my readers to give me a patient and indulgent hearing.

After all, I have great confidence in the honesty of Englishmen's minds. Truth is truth, however long it may be neglected. Facts are facts, however long they may lie buried. I only want to dig up some old facts which the sands of time have covered over, to bring to the light of day some old English monuments which have been long neglected, to unstop some old wells which the prince of this world has been diligently filling with earth. I ask my readers to give me their attention for a few minutes, and I trust to be able to show them that it is good to examine the question, "Why were our Reformers burned?"

I. The *broad facts* of the martyrdom of our Reformers are a story well known and soon told. But it may be useful to give a brief outline of these facts, in order to supply a framework to our subject.

Edward VI, "that incomparable young prince," as Bishop Burnet justly calls him, died on the 6th July, 1553. Never, perhaps, did any royal personage in this land die more truly lamented, or leave behind him a fairer reputation. Never, perhaps, to man's poor fallible judgment, did the cause of God's truth in England receive a heavier blow. His last prayer before death ought not to be forgotten, "O Lord God, defend this realm from papistry, and maintain Thy true religion." It was a prayer, I believe, not offered in vain.

After a foolish and deplorable effort to obtain the crown for Lady Jane Grey, Edward was succeeded by his eldest sister, Mary, daughter of Henry VIII and his first Queen, Catherine of Aragon, and best known in English history by the ill-omened name of "Bloody Mary." Mary had been brought up from her infancy as a rigid adherent of the Romish Church. She was, in fact, a very Papist of Papists, conscientious, zealous, bigoted, and narrow-minded in the extreme. She began at once to pull down her brother's work in every possible way, and to restore Popery in its worst and most offensive forms. Step by step she and her councillors marched back to Rome, trampling down one by one every obstacle, and as *thorough* as Lord Strafford in going straight forward to their mark. The Mass was restored; the English service was taken away; the works of Luther, Zwingli, Calvin, Tyndale, Bucer, Latimer, Hooper, and Cranmer were proscribed. Cardinal Pole was invited to England.

The foreign Protestants resident in England were banished. The leading divines of the Protestant Church of England were deprived of their offices, and, while some escaped to the Continent, many were put in prison. The old statutes against heresy were once more brought forward, primed and loaded. And thus by the beginning of 1555 the stage was cleared, and that bloody tragedy, in which Bishops Bonner and Gardiner played so prominent a part, was ready to begin.

For, unhappily for the credit of human nature, Mary's advisers were not content with depriving and imprisoning the leading English Reformers. It was resolved to make them abjure their principles, or to put them to death. One by one they were called before special Commissions, examined about their religious opinions, and called upon to recant, on pain of death if they refused. No third course, no alternative was left to them. They were either to give up Protestantism and receive Popery, or else they were to be burned alive. Refusing to recant, they were one by one handed over to the secular power, publicly brought out and chained to stakes, publicly surrounded with faggots, and publicly sent out of the world by that most cruel and painful of deaths, the death by fire. All these are broad facts which all the apologists of Rome can never gainsay or deny.

It is a broad fact that during the last four years of Queen Mary's reign no less than 288 persons were burnt at the stake for their adhesion to the Protestant faith.

In 1555 there were burnt	71
,, 1556	,,	89
,, 1557	,,	88
,, 1558	,,	40
		288[1]

Indeed, the faggots never ceased to blaze whilst Mary was alive, and five martyrs were burnt in Canterbury only a week before her

[1] These numbers are given by Soames, in his History of the Reformation (vol. iv. p. 587), and are taken from Strype. Some historians give higher numbers.

death. Out of these 288 sufferers, be it remembered, one was an archbishop, four were bishops, twenty-one were clergymen, fifty-five were women, and four were children.

It is a broad fact that these 288 sufferers were not put to death for any offence against property or person. They were not rebels against the Queen's authority, caught red-handed in arms. They were not thieves, or murderers, or drunkards, or unbelievers, or men and women of immoral lives. On the contrary, they were, with barely an exception, some of the holiest, purest, and best Christians in England, and several of them the most learned men of their day.

I might say much about the gross injustice and unfairness with which they were treated at their various examinations. Their trials, if indeed they can be called trials, were a mere mockery of justice. I might say much about the abominable cruelty with which most of them were treated, both in prison and at the stake. But you must read Foxe's Martyrs on these points. I make no comment on the stupid impolicy of the whole persecution. Never did Rome do herself such irreparable damage as she did in Mary's reign. Even unlearned people, who could not argue much, saw clearly that a Church which committed such horrible bloodshed could hardly be the one true Church of Christ![1] but I have no time for all this. I must conclude this general sketch of this part of my subject with two short remarks.

For one thing, I ask my readers never to forget that for the burning of our Reformers the Church of Rome is wholly and entirely responsible. The attempt to transfer the responsibility from the Church to the secular power is a miserable and dishonest subterfuge. The men of Judah did not slay Samson; but they delivered him bound into the hands of the Philistines! The Church of Rome did not slay the Reformers; but she condemned them, and the secular power executed the condemnation! The precise measure of responsibility which ought to be meted out to each of Rome's agents in the matter is a point that I do not care to settle. Miss Strickland, in her "Lives of the Queens of England," has tried in vain to shift the blame from unhappy Mary. With all the zeal of a woman, she has laboured hard to whitewash her

[1] A lady in high position told Bonner in a letter, after Philpot's death, that his cruelty had lost the hearts of 20,000 Papists in twelve months.

character. The reader of her biography will find little about martyrdoms. But it will not do. Mr Froude's volume tells a very different tale. The Queen, and her Council, and the Parliament, and the Popish Bishops, and Cardinal Pole, must be content to share the responsibility among them. One thing alone is very certain. They will never succeed in shifting the responsibility off the shoulders of the Church of Rome. Like the Jews and Pontius Pilate, when our Lord was crucified, all parties must bear the blame. THE BLOOD is upon them all.

For another thing, I wish my readers to remember that the burning of the Marian martyrs is an act that the Church of Rome has never repudiated, apologized for, or repented of, down to the present day. There stands the huge blot on her escutcheon; and there stands the huge fact side by side, that she never made any attempt to wipe it away. Never has she repented of her treatment of the Vaudois and the Albigenses; never has she repented of the wholesale murders of the Spanish Inquisition; never has she repented of the massacre of St Bartholomew; never has she repented of the burning of the English Reformers. We should make a note of that fact, and let it sink down into our minds. Rome never changes. Rome will never admit that she has made mistakes. She burned our English Reformers 300 years ago. She tried hard to stamp out by violence the Protestantism which she could not prevent spreading by arguments. If Rome had only the power, I am not sure that she would not attempt to play the whole game over again.

II. The question may now arise in our minds, *Who were the leading English Reformers* that were burned? What were their names, and what were the circumstances attending their deaths? These are questions which may very properly be asked, and questions to which I proceed at once to give an answer.

In this part of my paper I am very sensible that I shall seem to many to go over old ground. But I am bold to say that it is ground which ought often to be gone over. I, for one, want the names of our martyred Reformers to be "household words" in every Protestant family throughout the land. I shall, therefore, make no apology for giving the names of the nine principal English martyrs in the chronological order of their deaths, and for supplying you with a few facts about each of them. Never, I believe, since Christ left the world, did Christian men ever meet a cruel death with such glorious faith, and hope, and patience, as these Marian martyrs. Never did dying men leave behind them such a rich store of noble sayings, sayings which deserve to be written in golden letters in our histories, and handed down to our children's children.

(1) The first leading English Reformer who broke the ice and crossed the river, as a martyr in Mary's reign, was *John Rogers*, a London Minister, Vicar of St Sepulchre, and Prebendary and Reader of Divinity at St Paul's. He was burned in Smithfield on Monday, the 4th of February, 1555. Rogers was born at Deritend, in the parish of Aston, near Birmingham. He was a man who, in one respect, had done more for the cause of Protestantism than any of his fellow-sufferers. In saying this I refer to the fact that he had assisted Tyndale and Coverdale in bringing out a most important version of the English Bible, a version commonly known as Matthew's Bible. Indeed, he was condemned as "Rogers, *alias* Matthew." This circumstance, in all human probability, made him a marked man, and was one cause why he was the first who was brought to the stake.

Rogers' examination before Gardiner gives us the idea of his being a bold, thorough Protestant, who had fully made up his mind on all points of the Romish controversy, and was able to give a reason for his opinions. At any rate, he seems to have silenced and abashed his examiners even more than most of the martyrs did. But argument, of course, went for nothing. "Woe to the conquered!" If he had the Word, his enemies had the sword.[1]

On the morning of his martyrdom he was roused hastily in his cell in Newgate, and hardly allowed time to dress himself. He was then led forth to Smithfield on foot, within sight of the Church of St Sepulchre, where he had preached, and through the streets of the parish where he had done the work of a pastor. By the wayside

---

[1] Rogers' prophetic words in prison, addressed to Day, printer of Foxe's "Acts and Monuments," are well worth quoting: "Thou shalt live to see the alteration of this religion, and the Gospel freely preached again. Therefore, have me commended to my brethren, as well in exile as others, and bid them be circumspect in displacing the Papists and putting good ministers into Churches, or else their end will be worse than ours." *Foxe*, iii. p. 107 (1684 edition).

stood his wife and ten children (one a baby) whom Bishop Bonner, in his diabolical cruelty, had flatly refused him leave to see in prison. He just saw them, but was hardly allowed to stop, and then walked on calmly to the stake, repeating the 51st Psalm. An immense crowd lined the street, and filled every available spot in Smithfield. Up to that day men could not tell how English Reformers would behave in the face of death, and could hardly believe that Prebendaries and Dignitaries would actually give their bodies to be burned for their religion. But when they saw John Rogers, the first martyr, walking steadily and unflinchingly into a fiery grave, the enthusiasm of the crowd knew no bounds. They rent the air with thunders of applause. Even Noailles, the French Ambassador, wrote home a description of the scene, and said that Rogers went to death "as if he was walking to his wedding." By God's great mercy he died with comparative ease. And so the first Marian martyr passed away.

(2) The second leading Reformer who died for Christ's truth in Mary's reign was *John Hooper*, Bishop of Gloucester. He was burned at Gloucester on Saturday, the 9th of February, 1555.

Hooper was a Somersetshire man by birth. In many respects he was, perhaps, the noblest martyr of them all. Of all Edward the Sixth's bishops, none has left behind him a higher reputation for personal holiness, and diligent preaching and working in his diocese. None, judging from his literary remains, had clearer and more Scriptural views on all points in theology. Some might say that Edward the Sixth's Bishop of Gloucester was too Calvinistic; but he was not more so than the Thirty-nine Articles. Hooper was a far-sighted man, and saw the danger of leaving nest-eggs for Romanism in the Church of England. In his famous dispute with Cranmer and the other bishops about wearing Romish vestments at his consecration, it has been, I know, the fashion to condemn him as too stiff and unbending. I say boldly that the subsequent history of our Church makes it doubtful whether we ought not to reverse our verdict. The plain truth is, that in principle Hooper was right, and his opponents were wrong.

A man like Hooper, firm, stern, not naturally genial, unbending and unsparing in his denunciation of sin, was sure to have many enemies. He was one of the first marked for destruction as soon as Popery was restored. He was summoned to London at a very early stage of the Marian persecution, and, after lingering eighteen months in prison, and going through the form of examination by Bonner, Gardiner, Tunstall, and Day, was degraded from his office, and sentenced to be burned as a heretic.

At first it was fully expected that he would suffer in Smithfield with Rogers. This plan, for some unknown reason, was given up, and to his great satisfaction Hooper was sent down to Gloucester, and burnt in his own diocese, and in sight of his own cathedral. On his arrival there, he was received with every sign of sorrow and respect by a vast multitude, who went out on the Cirencester Road to meet him, and was lodged for the night in the house of a Mr Ingram, which is still standing, and probably not much altered. There Sir Anthony Kingston, whom the good Bishop had been the means of converting from a sinful life, entreated him, with many tears, to spare himself, and urged him to remember that "Life was sweet, and death was bitter." To this the noble martyr returned this memorable reply, that "Eternal life was more sweet, and eternal death was more bitter."

On the morning of his martyrdom he was led forth, walking, to the place of execution, where an immense crowd awaited him. It was market-day; and it was reckoned that nearly 7,000 people were present. The stake was planted directly in front of the western gate of the Cathedral-close, and within 100 yards of the deanery and the east front of the Cathedral. The exact spot is marked now by a beautiful memorial at the east end of the churchyard of St Mary-de-Lode. The window over the gate, where Popish friars watched the Bishop's dying agonies, stands unaltered to this day.

When Hooper arrived at this spot, he was allowed to pray, though strictly forbidden to speak to the people. And there he knelt down, and prayed a prayer which has been preserved and recorded by Foxe, and is of exquisitely touching character. Even then a box was put before him containing a full pardon, if he would only recant. His only answer was, "Away with it; if you love my soul, away with it!" He was then fastened to the stake by an iron round his waist, and fought his last fight with the king of terrors. Of all the martyrs, none perhaps, except Ridley, suffered more than Hooper did. Three times the faggots had to be lighted, because they would not burn properly. Three quarters of an hour the noble sufferer endured the mortal agony, as Foxe says, "neither moving backward, forward, nor to any side," but only praying, "Lord Jesus, have mercy on me; Lord Jesus, receive my spirit;" and beating his breast with one hand till it was burned to a stump. And so the good Bishop of Gloucester passed away.

(3) The third leading Reformer who suffered in Mary's reign was *Rowland Taylor*, Rector of Hadleigh, in Suffolk. He was burned on Aldham Common, close to his own parish, the same day that Hooper died at Gloucester, on Saturday, the 9th February, 1555.

Rowland Taylor is one of whom we know little, except that he was a great friend of Cranmer, and a doctor of divinity and canon law. But that he was a man of high standing among the Reformers is evident, from his being ranked by his enemies with Hooper, Rogers, and Bradford; and that he was an exceedingly able and ready divine is clear from his examination, recorded by Foxe. Indeed, there is hardly any of the sufferers about whom the old Martyrologist has gathered together so many touching and striking things. One might think he was a personal friend.

Striking was the reply which he made to his friends at Hadleigh, who urged him to flee, as he might have done, when he was first summoned to appear in London before Gardiner:

"What will ye have me to do? I am now old, and have already lived too long, to see these terrible and most wicked days. Fly you, and do as your conscience leadeth you. I am fully determined, with God's grace, to go to the Bishop and tell him to his beard that he doth naught. I believe before God that I shall never be able to do for my God such good service as I may do now." *Foxe's* "Acts and Monuments," vol. iii. p. 138.

Striking were the replies which he made to Gardiner and his other examiners. None spoke more pithily, weightily, and powerfully than did this Suffolk incumbent.

Striking and deeply affecting was his last testament and legacy of advice to his wife, his family, and parishioners, though far too long to be inserted here, excepting the last sentence:

"For God's sake beware of Popery: for though it appear to have in it unity, yet the same is vanity and antichristianity, and not in Christ's faith and verity." *Foxe's* "Acts and Monuments," vol. iii. p. 144.

He was sent down from London to Hadleigh, to his great delight, to be burned before the eyes of his parishioners. When he got within two miles of Hadleigh, the Sheriff of Suffolk asked him how he felt. "God be praised, Master Sheriff," was his reply, "never better. For now I am almost at home. I lack but just two stiles to go over, and I am even at my Father's house."

As he rode through the streets of the little town of Hadleigh, he found them lined with crowds of his parishioners, who had heard of his approach, and came out of their houses to greet him with many tears and lamentations. To them he only made one constant address, "I have preached to you God's Word and truth, and am come this day to seal it with my blood."

On coming to Aldham Common, where he was to suffer, they told him where he was. Then he said, "Thank God, I am even at home."

When he was stripped to his shirt and ready for the stake, he said, with a loud voice, "Good people, I have taught you nothing but God's Holy Word, and those lessons that I have taken out of the Bible; and I am come hither to seal it with my blood." He would probably have said more, but, like all the other martyrs, he was strictly forbidden to speak, and even now was struck violently on the head for saying these few words. He then knelt down and prayed, a poor woman of the parish insisting, in spite of every effort to prevent her, in kneeling down with him. After this, he was chained to the stake, and repeating the 51st Psalm, and crying to God, "Merciful Father, for Jesus Christ's sake, receive my soul into Thy hands," stood quietly amidst the flames without crying or moving, till one of the guards dashed out his brains with a halberd. And so this good old Suffolk incumbent passed away.

(4) The fourth leading Reformer who suffered in Mary's reign was *Robert Ferrar*, Bishop of St David's, in Wales. He was burned at Carmarthen on Saturday, the 30th March, 1555. Little is known of this good man beyond the fact that he was born at Halifax, and was the last Prior of Nostell, in Yorkshire, an office which he surrendered in 1540. He was also Chaplain to Archbishop Cranmer and to the Protector Somerset, and to this influence he owed his elevation to the Episcopal bench. He was first imprisoned for various trivial and ridiculous charges on temporal matters, in the latter days of Edward the Sixth, after the fall of the Protector

Somerset, and afterwards was brought before Gardiner, with Hooper, Rogers, and Bradford, on the far more serious matter of his doctrine. The articles exhibited against him clearly show that in all questions of faith he was of one mind with his fellow-martyrs. Like Hooper and Taylor, he was condemned to be burned in the place where he was best known, and was sent down from London to Carmarthen. What happened there at his execution is related very briefly by Foxe, partly, no doubt, because of the great distance of Carmarthen from London in those pre-railway days; partly, perhaps, because most of those who saw Ferrar burned could speak nothing but Welsh. One single fact is recorded which shows the good Bishop's courage and constancy in a striking light. He had told a friend before the day of execution that if he saw him once stir in the fire from the pain of his burning, he need not believe the doctrines he had taught. When the awful time came, he did not forget his promise, and, by God's grace, he kept it well. He stood in the flames holding out his hands till they were burned to stumps, until a bystander in mercy struck him on the head, and put an end to his sufferings. And so the Welsh Bishop passed away.

(5) The fifth leading Reformer who suffered in Mary's reign was *John Bradford*, Prebendary of St Paul's, and Chaplain to Bishop Ridley. He was burned in Smithfield on Monday, July the 1st, 1555, at the age of forty-five. Few of the English martyrs, perhaps, are better known than Bradford, and none certainly deserve better their reputation. Strype calls Bradford, Cranmer, Ridley, and Latimer, the "four prime pillars" of the Reformed Church of England. He was by birth a Manchester man, and to the end of his life retained a strong interest in the district with which he was connected. At an early age his high talents commended him to the notice of men in high quarters, and he was appointed one of the six royal chaplains who were sent about England to preach up the doctrines of the Reformation. Bradford's commission was to preach in Lancashire and Cheshire, and he seems to have performed his duty with singular ability and success. He preached constantly in Manchester, Liverpool, Bolton, Bury, Wigan, Ashton, Stockport, Eccles, Prestwich, Middleton, and Chester, with great benefit to the cause of Protestantism, and with great effect on men's souls. The consequence was what might have been

expected. Within a month of Queen Mary's accession Bradford was in prison, and never left it until he was burned. His personal holiness, and his extraordinary reputation as a preacher, made him an object of great interest during his imprisonment, and immense efforts were made to pervert him from the Protestant faith. All these efforts, however, were in vain. As he lived, so he died.[1]

On the day of his execution he was led out from Newgate to Smithfield about nine o'clock in the morning, amid such a crowd of people as was never seen either before or after. A Mrs Honywood, who lived to the age of ninety-two, and died in 1620, remembered going to see him burned, and her shoes being trodden off by the crowd. Indeed, when he came to the stake the Sheriffs of London were so alarmed at the press that they would not allow him and his fellow-sufferer, Leaf, to pray as long as they wished. "Arise," they said, "and make an end; for the press of the people is great."

"At that word," says Foxe, "they both stood up upon their feet, and then Master Bradford took a faggot in his hands and kissed it, and so likewise the stake." When he came to the stake he held up his hands, and, looking up to heaven, said, "O England, England, repent thee of thy sins! Beware of idolatry; beware of false antichrists! Take heed they do not deceive you!" After that he turned to the young man Leaf, who suffered with him, and said, "Be of good comfort, brother; for we shall have a merry supper with the Lord this night." After that he spoke no more that man could hear, excepting that he embraced the reeds, and said, "Strait is the gate, and narrow is the way, that leadeth to eternal life, and few there be that find it." "He endured the flames," says Fuller, "as a fresh gale of wind in a hot summer day." And so, in the prime of life, he passed away.

(6 & 7) The sixth and seventh leading Reformers who suffered in Mary's reign were two whose names are familiar to every Englishman, *Nicholas Ridley*, Bishop of London, and *Hugh Latimer*,

---

[1] Bradford seems to have had a very strong feeling about the causes for which God permitted the Marian persecution. Writing to his mother from prison, he says: "Ye all know there never was more knowledge of God, and less godly living and true serving of God. God, therefore, is now come, and because He will not damn us with the world He punisheth us." *Foxe*, iii. p. 255.

once Bishop of Worcester. They were both burned at Oxford, back to back, at one stake, on the 16th of October, 1555. Ridley was born at Willimotiswick, in Northumberland, on the Borders. Latimer was born at Thurcaston, in Leicestershire. The history of these two great English Protestants is so well known to most people that I need not say much about it. Next to Cranmer, there can be little doubt that no two men did so much to bring about the establishment of the principles of the Reformation in England. Latimer, as an extraordinary popular preacher, and Ridley, as a learned man and an admirable manager of the Metropolitan diocese of London, have left behind them reputations which never have been surpassed. As a matter of course, they were among the first that Bonner and Gardiner struck at when Mary came to the throne, and were persecuted with relentless severity until their deaths.

How they were examined again and again by Commissioners about the great points in controversy between Protestants and Rome, how they were shamefully baited, teased, and tortured by every kind of unfair and unreasonable dealing, how they gallantly fought a good fight to the end, and never gave way for a moment to their adversaries, all these are matters with which I need not trouble my readers. Are they not all fairly chronicled in the pages of good old Foxe? I will only mention a few circumstances connected with their deaths.

On the day of their martyrdom they were brought separately to the place of execution, which was at the end of Broad Street, Oxford, close to Balliol College. Ridley arrived on the ground first, and seeing Latimer come afterwards, ran to him and kissed him, saying, "Be of good heart, brother; for God will either assuage the fury of the flames, or else strengthen us to abide it." They then prayed earnestly, and talked with one another, though no one could hear what they said. After this they had to listen to a sermon by a wretched renegade divine named Smith, and, being forbidden to make any answer, were commanded to make ready for death.

Ridley's last words before the fire was lighted were these, "Heavenly Father, I give Thee most hearty thanks that Thou hast called me to a profession of Thee even unto death. I beseech Thee, Lord God, have mercy on this realm of England, and deliver the same from all her enemies." Latimer's last words were like the blast of a trumpet, which rings even to this day, "Be of good comfort, Master Ridley, and play the man; we shall this day, by God's grace, light such a candle in England as I trust shall never be put out."

When the flames began to rise, Ridley cried out with a loud voice in Latin, "Into thy hands, O Lord, I commend my spirit: Lord, receive my spirit," and afterwards repeated these last words in English. Latimer cried as vehemently on the other side of the stake, "Father of heaven, receive my soul."

Latimer soon died. An old man, above eighty years of age, it took but little to set his spirit free from its earthly tenement. Ridley suffered long and painfully, from the bad management of the fire by those who attended the execution. At length, however, the flames reached a vital part of him, and he fell at Latimer's feet, and was at rest. And so the two great Protestant bishops passed away. "They were lovely and beautiful in their lives, and in death they were not divided."

(8) The eighth leading English Reformer who suffered in Mary's reign was *John Philpot*, Archdeacon of Winchester. He was burned in Smithfield on Wednesday, December the 18th, 1555. Philpot is one of the martyrs of whom we know little comparatively, except that he was born at Compton, in Hampshire, was of good family, and well connected, and had a very high reputation for learning. The mere fact that at the beginning of Mary's reign he was one of the leading champions of Protestantism in the mock discussions which were held in Convocation, is sufficient to show that he was no common man. The relentless virulence with which he was persecuted by Gardiner is easily accounted for, when we remember that Gardiner, when he was deposed from his See in Edward VI's time, was Bishop of Winchester, and would naturally regard his successor, Bishop Ponet, and all his officials, with intense hatred. A Popish bishop was not likely to spare a Protestant archdeacon.

The thirteen examinations of Philpot before the Popish bishops are given by Foxe at great length, and fill no less than one hundred and forty pages of one of the Parker Society volumes. The length to which they were protracted shows plainly how anxious his judges were to turn him from his principles. The skill with which the Archdeacon maintained his ground, alone and unaided, gives a most favourable impression of his learning, no less than of his courage and patience.

The night before his execution he received a message, while at supper in Newgate, to the effect that he was to be burned next day. He answered at once, "I am ready: God grant me strength and a joyful resurrection." He then went into his bedroom, and thanked God that he was counted worthy to suffer for His truth.

The next morning, at eight o'clock, the Sheriffs called for him, and conducted him to Smithfield. The road was foul and muddy, as it was the depth of winter, and the officers took him up in their arms to carry him to the stake. Then he said, merrily, alluding to what he had probably seen at Rome, when travelling in his early days, "What, will you make me a Pope? I am content to go to my journey's end on foot."

When he came into Smithfield, he kneeled down and said, "I will pay my vows in thee, O Smithfield." He then kissed the stake and said, "Shall I disdain to suffer at this stake, seeing my Redeemer did not refuse to suffer a most vile death on the cross for me?" After that, he meekly repeated the 106th, 107th, and 108th Psalms; and being chained to the stake, died very quietly. And so the good Archdeacon passed away.

(9) The ninth and last leading Reformer who suffered in Mary's reign was *Thomas Cranmer*, Archbishop of Canterbury. He was burned at Oxford, on the 21st of March, 1556. Cranmer was born at Aslockton, in Nottinghamshire. There is no name among the English martyrs so well known in history as his. There is none certainly in the list of our Reformers to whom the Church of England, on the whole, is so much indebted. He was only a mortal man, and had his weaknesses and infirmities, it must be admitted; but still, he was a great man, and a good man.

Cranmer, we must always remember, was brought prominently forward at a comparatively early period in the English Reformation, and was made Archbishop of Canterbury at a time when his views of religion were confessedly half-formed and imperfect. Whenever quotations from Cranmer's writings are brought forward by the advocates of semi-Romanism in the Church of England, you should always ask carefully to what period of his life those quotations belong. In forming your estimate of Cranmer, do not forget his antecedents. He was a man who had the honesty to grope his way into fuller light,,and to cast aside his early opinions and confess that he had changed his mind on many subjects. How few men have the courage to do this!

Cranmer maintained an unblemished reputation throughout the reigns of Henry VIII and Edward VI, although frequently placed in most delicate and difficult positions. Not a single man can be named in those days who passed through so much dirt, and yet came out of it so thoroughly undefiled.

Cranmer, beyond all doubt, laid the foundation of our present Prayer-book and Articles. Though not perhaps a brilliant man, he was a learned one, and a lover of learned men, and one who was always trying to improve everything around him. When I consider the immense difficulties he had to contend with, I often wonder that he accomplished what he did. Nothing, in fact, but his steady perseverance would have laid the foundation of our Formularies.

I say all these things in order to break the force of the great and undeniable fact that he was the only English Reformer who for a time showed the white feather, and for a time shrank from dying for the truth! I admit that he fell sadly. I do not pretend to extenuate his fall. It stands forth as an everlasting proof that the best of men are only men at the best. I only want my readers to remember that if Cranmer failed as no other Reformer in England failed, he also had done what certainly no other Reformer had done.

From the moment that Mary came to the English throne, Cranmer was marked for destruction. It is probable that there was no other English divine whom the unhappy Queen regarded with such rancour and hatred. She never forgot that her mother's divorce was brought about by Cranmer's advice, and she never rested till he was burned.

Cranmer was imprisoned and examined just like Ridley and Latimer. Like them, he stood his ground firmly before the Commissioners. Like them, he had clearly the best of the argument in all points that were disputed. But, like them, of course, he was pronounced guilty of heresy, condemned, deposed, and sentenced to be burned.

And now comes the painful fact that in the last month of

Cranmer's life his courage failed him, and he was persuaded to sign a recantation of his Protestant opinions. Flattered and cajoled by subtle kindness, frightened at the prospect of so dreadful a death as burning, tempted and led away by the devil, Thomas Cranmer fell, and put his hand to a paper in which he repudiated and renounced the principles of the Reformation, for which he had laboured so long.

Great was the sorrow of all true Protestants on hearing these tidings! Great was the triumphing and exultation of all Papists! Had they stopped here and set their noble victim at liberty, the name of Cranmer would probably have sunk and never risen again. But the Romish party, as God would have it, outwitted themselves. With fiendish cruelty they resolved to burn Cranmer, even after he had recanted. This, by God's providence, was just the turning point for Cranmer's reputation. Through the abounding grace of God he repented of his fall, and found mercy. Through the same abounding grace he resolved to die in the faith of the Reformation. And at last, through abounding grace, he witnessed such a bold confession in St Mary's, Oxford, that he confounded his enemies, filled his friends with thankfulness and praise, and left the world a triumphant martyr for Christ's truth.

I need hardly remind you how, on the 21st March, the unhappy Archbishop was brought out, like Samson in the hands of the Philistines, to make sport for his enemies, and to be a gazingstock to the world in St Mary's Church, at Oxford. I need hardly remind you how, after Dr Cole's sermon he was invited to declare his faith, and was fully expected to acknowledge publicly his alteration of religion, and his adhesion to the Church of Rome. I need hardly remind you how, with intense mental suffering, the Archbishop addressed the assembly at great length, and at the close suddenly astounded his enemies by renouncing all his former recantations, declaring the Pope to be Antichrist, and rejecting the Popish doctrine of the Real Presence. Such a sight was certainly never seen by mortal eyes since the world began!

But then came the time of Cranmer's triumph. With a light heart, and a clear conscience, he cheerfully allowed himself to be hurried to the stake amidst the frenzied outcries of his disappointed enemies. Boldly and undauntedly he stood up at the stake while the flames curled around him, steadily holding out his right hand in the fire, and saying, with reference to his having signed a recantation, "This unworthy right hand," and steadily holding up his left hand towards heaven.[1] Of all the martyrs, strange to say, none at the last moment showed more *physical* courage than Cranmer did. Nothing, in short, in all his life became him so well as the manner of his leaving it. Greatly he had sinned, but greatly he had repented. Like Peter he fell, but like Peter he rose again. And so passed away the first Protestant Archbishop of Canterbury.

I will not trust myself to make any comment on these painful and interesting histories. I have not time. I only wish my readers to believe that the half of these men's stories have not been told them, and that the stories of scores of men and women less distinguished by position might easily be added to them, quite as painful and quite as interesting.[2] But I will say boldly, that the men who were burned in this way were not men whose memories ought to be lightly passed over, or whose opinions ought to be lightly esteemed. Opinions for which "an army of martyrs" died ought not to be dismissed with scorn. To their faithfulness we owe the existence of the Reformed Church of England. Her foundations were cemented with their blood. To their courage we owe, in a great measure, our English liberty. They taught the land that it was worth while to die for free thought. Happy is the land which has had such citizens! Happy is the Church which has had such Reformers! Honour be to those who at Smithfield, Oxford, Gloucester, Carmarthen, and Hadleigh have raised stones of remembrance and memorial to the martyrs!

III. But I pass on to a point which I hold to be one of cardinal importance in the present day. The point I refer to is *the special*

[1] Soames is my authority for this statement about Cranmer's left hand. I can find it nowhere else. He also mentions, what other historians record, that when the fire had burned down to ashes, Cranmer's heart was found unconsumed and uninjured. *Soames'* "History of the Reformation," vol. iv. p. 544.

[2] The following martyrdoms are recommended to the special notice of all who possess Foxe's Book of Martyrs: Laurence Saunders, burned at Coventry; William Hunter, at Brentwood; Rawlins White, at Cardiff; George Marsh, at Chester; Thomas Hawkes, at Coggeshall; John Bland, at Canterbury; Alice Driver, at Ipswich; Rose Allen, at Colchester; Joan Waste, at Derby; Richard Woodman, at Lewes; Agnes Prest, at Exeter; Julius Palmer, at Newbury; John Noyes, at Laxfield, in Suffolk.

reason why our Reformers were burned. Great indeed would be our mistake if we supposed that they suffered for the vague charge of refusing submission to the Pope, or desiring to maintain the independence of the Church of England. Nothing of the kind! The principal reason why they were burned was because they refused one of the peculiar doctrines of the Romish Church. On that doctrine, in almost every case, hinged their life or death. If they admitted it, they might live; if they refused it, they must die.

The doctrine in question was the *real presence* of the body and blood of Christ in the consecrated elements of bread and wine in the Lord's Supper. Did they, or did they not believe that the body and blood of Christ were really, that is, corporally, literally, locally, and materially, present under the forms of bread and wine after the words of consecration were pronounced? Did they or did they not believe that the real body of Christ, which was born of the Virgin Mary, was present on the so-called altar so soon as the mystical words had passed the lips of the priest? Did they or did they not? That was the simple question. If they did not believe and admit it, they were burned.[1]

There is a wonderful and striking unity in the stories of our martyrs on this subject. Some of them, no doubt, were attacked about the marriage of priests. Some of them were assaulted about the nature of the Catholic Church. Some of them were assailed on other points. But all, without an exception, were called to special account about the *real presence*, and in every case their refusal to admit the doctrine formed one principal cause of their condemnation.

(1) Hear what Rogers said:

"I was asked whether I believed in the sacrament to be the very body and blood of our Saviour Christ that was born of the Virgin Mary, and hanged on the cross, really and substantially? I answered, 'I think it to be false. I cannot understand really and substantially to signify otherwise

[1] "The Mass was one of the principal causes why so much turmoil was made in the Church, with the bloodshed of so many godly men." *Foxe's Preface to* vol. iii *of* "Acts and Monuments."

"The sacrament of the altar was the main touchstone to discover the poor Protestants. This point of the real, corporal presence of Christ in the sacrament, the same body that was crucified, was the compendious way to discover those of the opposite opinion." *Fuller*, "Church History," vol. iii. p. 399. Tegg's edition.

than corporally. But corporally Christ is only in heaven, and so Christ cannot be corporally in your sacrament.' " *Foxe in loco*, vol. iii. p. 101, edition, 1684.

And therefore he was condemned and burned.

(2) Hear what Bishop Hooper said:

"Tunstall asked him to say, 'whether he believed the corporal presence in the sacrament,' and Master Hooper said plainly 'that there was none such, neither did he believe any such thing.' Whereupon they bade the notaries write that he was married and would not go from his wife, and that he believed not the corporal presence in the sacrament; wherefore he was worthy to be deprived of his bishopric." *Foxe in loco*, vol. iii. p. 123.

And so he was condemned and burned.

(3) Hear what Rowland Taylor said:

"The second cause why I was condemned as a heretic is that I denied transubstantiation, and concomitation, two juggling words whereby the Papists believe that Christ's natural body is made of bread, and the Godhead by and by to be joined thereto, so that immediately after the words of consecration, there is no more bread and wine in the sacrament, but the substance only of the body and blood of Christ."

"Because I denied the aforesaid Papistical doctrine (yea, rather, plain, most wicked idolatry, blasphemy, and heresy) I was judged a heretic." *Foxe in loco*, vol. iii. p. 141.

And therefore he was condemned and burned.

(4) Hear what was done with Bishop Ferrar.

He was summoned to "grant the natural presence of Christ in the sacrament under the form of bread and wine," and because he refused to subscribe this article as well as others, he was condemned. And in the sentence of condemnation it is finally charged against him that he maintained that "the sacrament of the altar ought not to be ministered on an altar, or to be elevated, or to be adored in any way." *Foxe in loco*, vol. iii. p. 178.

And so he was burned.

(5) Hear what holy John Bradford wrote to the men of Lancashire and Cheshire when he was in prison:

"The chief thing which I am condemned for as an heretic is because I deny in the sacrament of the altar (which is not Christ's Supper, but a plain perversion as the Papists now use it) to be a real, natural, and corporal presence of Christ's body and blood under the forms and accidents of bread and wine: that is, because I deny transubstantiation, which is the darling of the devil, and daughter and heir to Antichrist's religion." *Foxe in loco*, vol. iii. p. 260.

And so he was condemned and burned.

(6) Hear what were the words of the sentence of condemnation against Bishop Ridley:

"The said Nicholas Ridley affirms, maintains, and stubbornly defends certain opinions, assertions, and heresies, contrary to the Word of God and the received faith of the Church, as in denying the true and natural body and blood of Christ to be in the sacrament of the altar, and secondarily, in affirming the substance of bread and wine to remain after the words of consecration." *Foxe in loco*, vol. iii. p. 426.

And so he was condemned and burned.

(7) Hear the articles exhibited against Bishop Latimer:

"That thou hast openly affirmed, defended, and maintained that the true and natural body of Christ after the consecration of the priest, is not really present in the sacrament of the altar, and that in the sacrament of the altar remaineth still the substance of bread and wine."

And to this article the good old man replied:

"After a corporal being, which the Romish Church prescribeth, Christ's body and blood is not in the sacrament under the forms of bread and wine." *Foxe in loco*, vol. iii. p. 426

And so he was condemned and burned.

(8) Hear the address made by Bishop Bonner to Archdeacon Philpot:

"You have offended and trespassed against the sacrament of the altar, denying the real presence of Christ's body and blood to be there, affirming also material bread and material wine to be in the sacrament, and not the substance of the body and blood of Christ." *Foxe in loco*, vol. iii. p. 495.

And because the good man stoutly adhered to this opinion he was condemned and burned.

(9) Hear, lastly, what Cranmer said with almost his last breath, in St Mary's Church, Oxford:

"As for the sacrament, I believe, as I have taught in my book against the Bishop of Winchester, the which my book teacheth so true a doctrine, that it shall stand at the last day before the judgment of God when the Papist's doctrine contrary thereto shall be ashamed to show her face." *Foxe in loco*, vol. iii. p. 562.

If any one wants to know what Cranmer had said in this book, let him take the following sentence as a specimen:

"They (the Papists) say that Christ is corporally under or in the forms of bread and wine. We say that Christ is not there, *neither corporally nor spiritually*; but in them that worthily eat and drink the bread and wine He is spiritually, and corporally in heaven." "Cranmer on the Lord's Supper." Parker Society edition, p. 54.

And so he was burned.

Now, were the English Reformers right in being so stiff and unbending on this question of the *real presence*? Was it a point of such vital importance that they were justified in dying before they would receive it? These are questions, I suspect, which are very puzzling to many unreflecting minds. Such minds, I fear, can see in the whole controversy about the real presence nothing but a logomachy, or strife of words. But they are questions, I am bold to say, on which no well-instructed Bible reader can hesitate for a moment in giving his answer. Such an one will say at once that the Romish doctrine of the *real presence* strikes at the very root of the Gospel, and is the very citadel and keep of Popery. Men may not see this at first, but it is a point that ought to be carefully remembered. It throws a clear and broad light on the line which the Reformers took, and the unflinching firmness with which they died.

Whatever men please to think or say, the Romish doctrine of the *real presence*, if pursued to its legitimate consequences, obscures every leading doctrine of the Gospel, and damages and interferes with the whole system of Christ's truth. Grant for a moment that the Lord's Supper is a sacrifice, and not a sacrament—grant that every time the words of consecration are used the natural body and blood of Christ are present on the Communion Table under the forms of bread and wine—grant that every one who eats that consecrated bread and drinks that consecrated wine does really eat and drink the natural body and blood of Christ—grant for a moment these things, and then see what momentous consequences result from these premises. You spoil the blessed doctrine of *Christ's finished work* when He died on the cross. A sacrifice that needs to be repeated is not a perfect and complete thing. You spoil the *priestly office* of Christ. If there are priests that can offer an acceptable sacrifice of God besides Him, the great High Priest is robbed of His glory. You spoil the Scriptural doctrine of the *Christian ministry*. You exalt sinful men into the position of mediators between God and man. You give to the sacramental elements of bread and wine an honour and veneration they were never meant to receive, and produce an *idolatry* to be abhorred of faithful Christians. Last, but not least, you overthrow the true doctrine of *Christ's human nature*. If the body born of the Virgin Mary can be in more places than one at the same time, it is not a body like our own, and Jesus was not "the second Adam" in the truth of our nature. I cannot doubt for a moment that our martyred Reformers saw and felt these things even more clearly than we do, and, seeing and feeling them, chose to die rather than admit the doctrine of the real presence. Feeling them, they would not give way by subjection for a moment, and cheerfully laid down their lives. Let this fact be deeply graven in our minds. Wherever the English language is spoken on the face of the globe this fact ought to be clearly understood by every Englishman who reads history. Rather than admit the doctrine of the real presence of Christ's natural body and blood under the forms of bread and wine, the Reformers of the Church of England were content to be burned.

IV. And now I must ask the special attention of my readers while I try to show the *bearing of the whole subject on our own position and on our own times*. I must ask you to turn from the dead to the living, to look away from England in 1555 to England in this present enlightened and advanced age, and to consider seriously the light which the burning of our Reformers throws on the Church of England at the present day.

We live in momentous times. The ecclesiastical horizon on every side is dark and lowering. The steady rise and progress of extreme Ritualism and Ritualists are shaking the Church of England to its very centre. It is of the very first importance to understand clearly what it all means. A right diagnosis of disease is the very first element of successful treatment. The physician who does not see what is the matter is never likely to work any cures.

Now, I say there can be no greater mistake than to suppose that the great controversy of our times is a mere question of vestments and ornaments—of chasubles and copes—of more or less church decorations—of more or less candles and flowers—of more or less bowings and turnings and crossings—of more or less gestures and postures—of more or less show and form. The man who fancies that the whole dispute is a mere æsthetic one, a question of taste, like one of fashion and millinery, must allow me to tell him that he is under a complete delusion. He may sit on the shore, like the Epicurean philosopher, smiling at theological storms, and flatter himself that we are only squabbling about trifles; but I take leave to tell him that his philosophy is very shallow, and his knowledge of the controversy of the day very superficial indeed.

The things I have spoken of are *trifles*, I fully concede. But they are pernicious trifles, because they are the outward expression of an inward doctrine. They are the skin disease which is the symptom of an unsound constitution. They are the plague spot which tells of internal poison. They are the curling smoke which arises from a hidden volcano of mischief. I, for one, would never make any stir about church millinery, or incense, or candles, if I thought they meant nothing beneath the surface. But I believe they mean a great deal of error and false doctrine, and therefore I publicly protest against them, and say that those who support them are to be blamed.

I give it as my deliberate opinion that the root of the whole Ritualistic system is the dangerous doctrine of the real presence of Christ's natural body and blood in the Lord's Supper under the forms of the consecrated bread and wine. If words mean anything, this *real presence* is the foundation principle of Ritualism. This *real presence* is what the extreme members of the Ritualistic party want to bring back into the Church of England. And just as our martyred Reformers went to the stake rather than admit the real presence, so I hold that we should make any sacrifice and contend to the bitter end, rather than allow a materialistic doctrine about Christ's presence in the Lord's Supper to come back in any shape into our Communion.

I will not weary my readers with quotations in proof of what I affirm. They have heard enough, perhaps too much, of them. But I must ask permission to give two short extracts.

Observe what Dr Pusey says, in a sermon called "Will ye also go away?" (Parker's, 1867):

"While repudiating any materialistic conceptions of the mode of the presence of our Lord in the Holy Eucharist, such as I believe is condemned in the term 'corporal presence of our Lord's flesh and blood,' *i.e.*, as though His precious body and blood were present in any gross or carnal way, and not rather sacramentally, really, spiritually—I believe that in the Holy Eucharist the body and blood of Christ are sacramentally, supernaturally, ineffably, but verily and indeed present, 'under the forms of bread and wine;' and that 'where His body is, there is Christ.' "

Observe what Dr Littledale says, in a tract called "The Real Presence":

"I. The Christian Church teaches, and has always taught, that in the Holy Communion, after consecration, the body and blood of the Lord Jesus Christ are 'verily and indeed' present on the altar under the forms of bread and wine.

"II. The Church also teaches that this presence depends on God's will, not on man's belief, and therefore that bad and good people receive the very same thing in communicating, the good for their benefit, the bad for their condemnation.

"III. Further, that as Christ is both God and Man, and as these two natures are for ever joined in His one person, His Godhead must be wherever His body is, and therefore He is to be worshipped in His sacrament.

"IV. The body and blood present are that same body and blood which were conceived by the Holy Ghost, born of the Virgin Mary, suffered under Pontius Pilate, ascended into heaven, but they are not present in the *same manner* as they were when Christ walked on earth. He, as Man, is now *naturally* in heaven, there to be till the last day, yet He is *supernaturally*, and just as truly, present in the Holy Communion, in some way which we cannot explain, but only believe."

In both these quotations, we may observe, there is an attempt to evade the charge of maintaining a "gross and carnal presence." The attempt, however, is not successful. It is a very curious fact that the Romish controversialist, Mr Harding, Bishop Jewell's opponent, said just as much 300 years ago. He said:

"Christ's body is present not after a corporal, or carnal, or naturally wise, but invisibly, unspeakably, miraculously, supernaturally, spiritually, Divinely, and in a manner by Him known." "Harding's Reply to Jewell," p. 434. Parker Society edit.

In both cases we can hardly fail to observe that the very expression which our martyrs steadily refused is employed, "present under the forms of bread and wine."

It is clear, to my mind, that if Dr Pusey and Dr Littledale had been brought before Gardiner and Bonner three hundred years ago, they would have left the court with flying colours, and, at any rate, would not have been burned.

I might refer my readers to the other published sermons on the Lord's Supper by men of high position in our Church. I might refer them to several Ritualistic manuals for the use of Communicants. I might refer them to the famous book "Directorium Anglicanum." I simply give it as my opinion that no plain man in his senses can read the writings of extreme Ritualists about the Lord's Supper and see any real distinction between the doctrine they hold and downright Popery. It is a distinction without a difference, and one that any jury of twelve honest men would say at once could not be proved.

I turn from books and sermons to churches, and I ask any reflecting mind to mark, consider, and digest what may be seen in any thorough-going Ritualistic place of worship. I ask him to mark the superstitious veneration and idolatrous honour with which everything within the chancel, and around and upon the

Lord's table, is regarded. I boldly ask any jury of twelve honest and unprejudiced men to look at that chancel and communion table, and tell me what they think all this means. I ask them whether the whole thing does not savour of the Romish doctrine of the Real Presence, and the sacrifice of the Mass? I believe that if Bonner and Gardiner had seen the chancels and communion tables of some of the churches of this day, they would have lifted up their hands and rejoiced; while Ridley, Bishop of London, and Hooper, Bishop of Gloucester, would have turned away with righteous indignation and said, "This communion table is not meant for the Lord's Supper on the Lord's board, but for counterfeiting the idolatrous Popish Mass."

I do not for a moment deny the zeal, earnestness, and sincerity of the extreme Ritualists, though as much might be said for the Pharisees or the Jesuits. I do not deny that we live in a singularly free country, and that Englishmen, now-a-days, have liberty to commit any folly short of "felo-de-se." But I do deny that any clergyman, however zealous and earnest, has a right to re-introduce Popery into the Church of England. And, above all, I deny that he has any right to maintain the very principle of the Real Presence, for opposing which the Reformers of his Church were burned.

The plain truth is, that the doctrine of the extreme Ritualistic school about the Lord's Supper can never be reconciled with the dying opinions of our martyred Reformers. The members of this school may protest loudly that they are sound churchmen, but they certainly are not churchmen of the same opinions as the Marian martyrs. If words mean anything, Hooper, and Rogers, and Ridley, and Bradford, and their companions, held one view of the Real Presence, and the ultra-Ritualists hold quite another. If they were right, the Ritualists are wrong. There is a gulf that cannot be crossed between the two parties. There is a thorough difference that cannot be reconciled or explained away. If we hold with one side, we cannot possibly hold with the other. For my part, I say, unhesitatingly, that I have more faith in Ridley, and Hooper, and Bradford, than I have in all the leaders of the ultra-Ritualistic party.

But what are we going to do? The danger is very great, far greater, I fear, than most people suppose. A conspiracy has been long at work for *unprotestantizing* the Church of England, and all the energies of Rome are concentrated on this little island. A sapping and mining process has been long going on under our feet, of which we are beginning at last to see a little. We shall see a good deal more by and by. At the rate we are going, it would never surprise me if within fifty years the crown of England were no longer on a Protestant head, and High Mass were once more celebrated in Westminster Abbey and St Paul's. The danger, in plain words, is neither more nor less than that of our Church being unprotestantized and going back to Babylon and Egypt. We are in imminent peril of re-union with Rome.

Men may call me an alarmist, if they like, for using such language. But I reply, there is a cause. The upper classes in this land are widely infected with a taste for a sensuous, histrionic, formal religion. The lower orders are becoming sadly familiarized with all the ceremonialism which is the stepping-stone to Popery. The middle classes are becoming disgusted with the Church of England, and asking what is the use of it. The intellectual classes are finding out that all religions are either equally good or equally bad. The House of Commons will do nothing unless pressed by public opinion. We have no Pyms or Hampdens there now. And all this time Ritualism grows and spreads. The ship is among breakers, breakers ahead and breakers astern, breakers on the right hand and breakers on the left. Something needs to be done, if we are to escape shipwreck.

The very life of the Church of England is at stake, and nothing less. Take away the Gospel from a Church and that Church is not worth preserving. A well without water, a scabbard without a sword, a steam-engine without a fire, a ship without compass and rudder, a watch without a mainspring, a stuffed carcase without life, all these are useless things. But there is nothing so useless as a Church without the Gospel. And this is the very question that stares us in the face. Is the Church of England to retain the Gospel or not? Without it in vain shall we turn to our archbishops and bishops, in vain shall we glory in our cathedrals and parish churches. Ichabod will soon be written on our walls. The ark of God will not be with us. Surely something ought to be done.

One thing, however, is very clear to my mind. We ought not lightly to forsake the Church of England. No! so long as her

Articles and Formularies remain unaltered, unrepealed, and unchanged, so long we ought not to forsake her. Cowardly and base is that seaman who launches the boat and forsakes the ship so long as there is a chance of saving her. Cowardly, I say, is that Protestant Churchman who talks of seceding because things on board our Church are at present out of order. What though some of the crew are traitors, and some are asleep! What though the old ship has some leaks, and her rigging has given way in some places! Still I maintain there is much to be done. There is life in the old ship yet. The great Pilot has not yet forsaken her. The compass of the Bible is still on deck. There are yet left on board some faithful and able seamen. So long as the Articles and Formularies are not Romanized, let us stick by the ship. So long as she has Christ and the Bible, let us stand by her to the last plank, nail our colours to the mast, and never haul them down. Once more, I say, let us not be wheedled, or bullied, or frightened, or cajoled, or provoked, into forsaking the Church of England

In the name of the Lord let us set up our banners. If ever we would meet Ridley and Latimer and Hooper in another world without shame, let us "contend earnestly" for the truths which they died to preserve. The Church of England expects every Protestant Churchman to do his duty. Let us not talk only, but act. Let us not act only, but pray. "He that hath no sword, let him sell his garment and buy one."

There is a voice in the blood of the martyrs. What does that voice say? It cries aloud from Oxford, Smithfield, and Gloucester, "Resist to the death the Popish doctrine of the Real Presence, under the forms of the consecrated bread and wine in the Lord's Supper!"

NOTE. The following quotations about the doctrine of the "Real Presence" are commended to the special attention of all Churchmen in the present day:

(1) "Whereas it is ordained in this Office for the Administration of the Lord's Supper, that the Communicants should receive the same kneeling; (which order is well meant, for a signification of our humble and grateful acknowledgment of the benefits of Christ therein given to all worthy Receivers, and for the avoiding of such profanation and disorder in the Holy Communion, as might otherwise ensue;) yet, lest the same kneeling should by any persons, either out of ignorance and infirmity, or out of

malice and obstinacy, be misconstrued and depraved; It is hereby declared, That thereby no adoration is intended, or ought to be done, either unto the Sacramental Bread or Wine there bodily received, or unto any corporal presence of Christ's natural Flesh and Blood. For the Sacramental Bread and Wine remain still in their very natural substances, and therefore may not be adored; (for that were Idolatry, to be abhorred of all faithful Christians;) and the natural Body and Blood of our Saviour Christ are in Heaven, and not here; it being against the truth of Christ's natural Body to be at one time in more places than one." Rubric at the end of the Communion Service in the Book of Common Prayer.

(2) "As concerning the form of doctrine used in this Church of England in the Holy Communion, that the Body and Blood of Christ be under the forms of bread and wine, when you shall show the place where this form of words is expressed, then shall you purge yourself from that which in the meantime I take to be *a plain untruth*." "Cranmer's Answer to Gardiner," pp. 52, 53, Parker edition.

(3) "The real presence of Christ's most blessed Body and Blood is not to be sought for in the sacrament, but in the worthy receiver of the sacrament." "Hooker's Eccles. Pol.," Bk. v. p. 67.

(4) "The Church of England has wisely forborne to use the term of *Real Presence* in all the books set forth by her authority. We neither find it recommended in the Liturgy, nor the Articles, nor the Homilies, nor the Church Catechism, nor Nowell's Catechism. For though it be once in the Liturgy, and once more in the Articles of 1552, it is mentioned in both places as a phrase of the Papists, and rejected for their abuse of it. So that if any Church of England man use it, he does more than the Church directs him; if any reject it, he has the Church's example to warrant him." "Dean Aldrich's Reply," p. 13, 1684. See "Goode on Eucharist," p. 38.

JOHN HOOPER: BISHOP AND MARTYR

In a day of religious controversy, no one is so useful to his generation as the man who contributes a little "light." Amidst the din and strife of ecclesiastical warfare, amidst the fog and dust stirred up by excited disputants, amidst assertions and counter-assertions, a thinking man will often cry with the dying philosopher, "I want more light: give me more light." He that can make two ears of corn grow where only one grew before, has been rightly called a benefactor to mankind. He that can throw a few rays of fresh light on the theological questions of the day, is surely doing a service to the Church and the world.

Thoughts such as these came across my mind when I chose the subject of this biographical paper: "*John Hooper, the martyred Bishop of Gloucester: his times, life, death, and opinions.*" I chose it with a meaning. I have long felt that the lives and opinions of the English Reformers deserve attentive study in the present day. I think that a picture of John Hooper will throw useful light on points of deep interest in our times.

We live in days when the Romish Church is making gigantic efforts to regain her lost power in England, and thousands of English people are helping her. None are doing the work of Rome so thoroughly as that singular body of English Churchmen, the extreme Ritualists. Consciously or unconsciously, they are paving the way for her advance, and laying down the rails for her trains. They are familiarizing the minds of thousands with Romish ceremonial, its millinery, its processions, its gestures, its postures, its theatrical, sensuous style of worship. They are boldly preaching and publishing downright Romish doctrine, the Real Presence, the priestly character of the ministry, the necessity of auricular confession and sacerdotal absolution. They are loudly proclaiming their desire for re-union with the Church of Rome. In short, it seems as if the battle of the Reformation must be fought over again. Now before we go back to Rome, let us thoroughly understand what English Romanism was. Let us bring in the light. Let us not take a "leap in the dark."

We live in times when many Churchmen openly sneer at our Reformation, and scoff at our Reformers. The martyrs, whose blood was the seed of our Church, are abused and vilified, and declared to be no martyrs at all. Cranmer is called "a cowardly traitor," and Latimer, "a coarse, illiterate bully!" The Reformation is said to have been "an unmitigated disaster," and a "change taken in hand by a conspiracy of adulterers, murderers, and thieves!" (See *Church Times*, of March 14, 1867.) Let us study one of our leading Reformers to-day, and see what the man was like. Let us pass under review one who was a friend and contemporary of Cranmer, Ridley, and Latimer, and a leading fellow-labourer in the work of the Reformation. Let us find out how he lived, and how he preached, and what he thought, and how he died. Once more I say, let us bring in the light.

We live in times when the strangest misrepresentations prevail about the true character of the Church of England. Scores of people all over the country are not ashamed to denounce the very name of Protestantism, and to tell people that "Evangelical" Churchmen are not Churchmen at all! Forsooth, they are Calvinists, Puritans, Dissenters, Methodists, Fanatics, and the like, and ought to leave the Church of England and go to their own place! Let us bring these assertions to the test of a few plain facts.

Let us examine the recorded sentiments, the written opinions, of one of the very divines to whom we owe our Articles and Prayerbook, with very few alterations. Let us hear what Bishop Hooper wrote, and thought, and taught. Let us not hastily concede that Ritualists and High Churchmen are the true representatives of the Church of England. "He that is first in his own cause seemeth just, but his neighbour that cometh after searcheth him." (Prov. xviii. 17.) Once more, I say, let us turn on the light.

I. I will begin by giving some account of *Bishop Hooper's times*. What kind of times were they in a religious point of view? Out of the pages of Foxe, Strype, Burnet, Soames, and Blunt, let me try to supply a few historical gleanings.

John Hooper was born about 1495 and died in 1555. He first saw the light in the reign of Henry VII, and was burned in the reign of Queen Mary. He lived through the whole reigns of Henry VIII and Edward VI, and was an eyewitness of all that took place under the government of those two kings. The sixty years of his life take in one of the most eventful periods of English history. It would be impossible to exaggerate the difference there was between England in 1495 and the same England in 1555. In a religious and moral view, the whole country was turned upside down. When Hooper was born, the English Reformation had not begun, and the Church of Rome ruled England undisturbed. When he died, the Reformation had struck such deep root, that neither argument nor persecution could overthrow it.

What were the leading characteristics of English religion before the Reformation? In what state did the mighty change which Hooper witnessed, and helped forward, find our forefathers? In one word, what does England owe to that subversion of Popery and that introduction of Protestantism, in which Hooper was a leading instrument? Let me try to supply a short answer to these questions. They are subjects, I am sorry to say, on which most people seem to know nothing at all. The minds of the vast majority of my countrymen appear to be a total blank about the history of three hundred years ago. With all the stir made about education, the ignorance of our own country's history is something lamentable and appalling and depressing. I never can believe that extreme Ritualism would have obtained so many adherents, if English people only knew the extent of our debt to the Protestant Reformation. They would never trifle, and tamper, and dabble with Popery, if they only knew what Popery was.

(a) Before the Reformation, one leading feature of English religion was *dense ignorance*. There was among all classes a conspicuous absence of all knowledge of true Christianity. A gross darkness overspread the land, a darkness that might be felt. Not one in a hundred could have told you as much about the Gospel of Christ as we could now learn from any intelligent Sunday School child.

We need not wonder at this ignorance. The people had neither schools nor Bibles. Wickliffe's New Testament, the only translation extant till Henry VIII's Bible was printed, cost £2 16s. 3d. of our money. The prayers of the Church were in Latin, and of course the people could not understand them. Preaching there was scarcely any. Quarterly sermons indeed were prescribed to the clergy, but not insisted on. Latimer says that while Mass was never to be left unsaid for a single Sunday, sermons might be omitted for twenty Sundays, and nobody was blamed. After all, when there were sermons, they were utterly unprofitable: and latterly to be a preacher was to be suspected of being a heretic.

To cap all, the return that Hooper got from the diocese of Gloucester, when he was first appointed Bishop in 1551, will give a pretty clear idea of the ignorance of Pre-Reformation times. Out of 311 clergy of his diocese, 168 were unable to repeat the Ten Commandments; 31 of the 168 could not state in what part of Scripture they were to be found; 40 could not tell where the Lord's Prayer was written; and 31 of the 40 were ignorant who was the author of the Lord's Prayer!

If this is not ignorance, I know not what is. If such were the pastors, what must the people have been! If this was the degree of knowledge among the parsons, what must it have been among the people!

(b) But this is not all. Before the Reformation, another leading feature of English religion was *superstition of the lowest and most degrading description*. Of the extent to which this was carried few, I suspect, have the smallest idea.

Men and women in those days had uneasy consciences sometimes, and wanted relief. They had sorrow and sickness and death to pass through, just like ourselves. What could they do? Whither could they turn? There was none to tell them of the love of God and the mediation of Christ, of the glad tidings of free, full, and complete salvation, of justification by faith, of grace, and faith, and hope, and repentance. They could only turn to the priests, who knew nothing themselves and could tell nothing to others. "The blind led the blind, and both fell into the ditch." In a word, the religion of our ancestors, before Hooper's time, was little better than an organized system of Virgin Mary worship, saint worship, image worship, relic worship, pilgrimages, almsgivings, formalism, ceremonialism, processions, prostrations, bowings, crossings, fastings, confessions, absolutions, masses, penances, and blind obedience to the priests. It was a grand higgledy-piggledy of ignorance and idolatry, and service done to an unknown God by deputy. The only practical result was that the priests took the people's money, and undertook to ensure their salvation, and the people flattered themselves that the more they gave to the priests, the more sure they were of going to heaven.

The catalogue of gross and ridiculous impostures which the priests practised on the people would fill a volume, and I cannot of course do more than supply a few specimens.

At the Abbey of Hales, in Gloucestershire, a vial was shown by the priests to those who offered alms, which was said to contain the blood of Christ. On examination, in King Henry VIII's time, this notable vial was found to contain neither more nor less than the blood of a duck, which was renewed every week.[1]

At Bexley, in Kent, a crucifix was exhibited, which received peculiar honour and large offerings, because of a continual miracle which was said to attend its exhibition. When people offered copper, the face of the figure looked grave; when they offered silver, it relaxed its severity; when they offered gold, it openly smiled. In Henry VIII's time this famous crucifix was examined, and wires were found within it by which the priests could move the face of the image, and make it assume any expression that they pleased.

At Reading Abbey, in Berkshire, the following relics, among many others, were most religiously worshipped, an angel with one wing, the spear-head that pierced our Saviour's side, two pieces of the holy cross, St James' hand, St Philip's stole, and a bone of Mary Magdalene.

At Bury St Edmunds, in Suffolk, the priests exhibited the coals that roasted St Lawrence, the parings of St Edmund's toenails, Thomas à Becket's penknife and boots, and as many pieces of our Saviour's cross as would have made, if joined together, one large whole cross.

At Maiden Bradley Priory, in Somersetshire, the worshippers were privileged to see the Virgin Mary's smock, part of the bread

---

[1] It was much more likely to have been "honey clarified, and coloured with saffron", as explained in Remains of Latimer (Parker Society) p. 408.

used at the original Lord's Supper, and a piece of the stone manger in which our Lord was laid at Bethlehem.

At Bruton Priory, in Somersetshire, was kept a girdle of the Virgin Mary, made of red silk. This solemn relic was sent as a special favour to women in childbirth, to insure them a safe delivery. The like was done with a white girdle of Mary Magdalene, kept at Farley Abbey, in Wiltshire. In neither case, we may be sure, was the relic sent without a pecuniary consideration.[1]

Records like these are so silly and melancholy that one hardly knows whether to laugh or to cry. But it is positively necessary to bring them forward, in order that men may know what was the religion of our forefathers before the Reformation. Wonderful as these things may sound in our ears, we must never forget that Englishmen in those times knew no better. A famishing man, in sieges and blockades, has been known to eat mice and rats rather than die of hunger. A soul famishing for lack of God's Word must not be judged too harshly if it struggles to find comfort in the most grovelling superstition.

(c) One thing more yet remains behind. Before the Reformation, another leading feature of English religion was *wide-spread unholiness and immorality*. The lives of the clergy, as a general rule, were simply scandalous, and the moral tone of the laity was naturally at the lowest ebb. Of course grapes will never grow on thorns, nor figs on thistles. To expect the huge roots of ignorance and superstition, which filled our land, to bear any but corrupt fruit, would be unreasonable and absurd. But a more thoroughly corrupt set than the English clergy were, in the palmy days of undisturbed Romanism, it would be impossible to imagine.

I might tell you of the habits of gluttony, drunkenness, and gambling, for which the parochial priesthood became unhappily notorious.

"Too often," says Professor J. J. Blunt, in his excellent history of the Reformation, "they were persons taken from the lowest of the people, with all the gross habits of the class from which they sprang, loiterers on the alehouse bench, dicers, scarce able to read by rote their paternoster, often unable to repeat the ten commandments, mass-priests, who could just read their breviaries, and no more, men often dubbed by the uncomplimentary names

[1] Strype and Burnet are my authority for the above mentioned facts.

of Sir John Lack-Latin, Sir John Mumble-Matins, or babbling and blind Sir John. In fact, the carnal living, fat bellies, and general secularity of ministers of religion were proverbial before the Reformation."

I might tell you of the shameless covetousness which marked the Pre-Reformation priesthood. So long as a man gave liberal offerings at the shrine of such saints as Thomas à Becket, the clergy would absolve him of almost any sin. So long as a felon or malefactor paid the monks well, he might claim sanctuary within the precincts of religious houses, after any crime, and hardly any law could reach him. Yet all this time for Lollards and Wickliffites there was no mercy at all! The very carvings still extant in some old ecclesiastical buildings tell a story in stone and wood, which speaks volumes to this day. Friars were often represented as foxes preaching, with the neck of a stolen goose peeping out of the hood behind, as wolves giving absolution, with a sheep muffled up in their cloaks, as apes sitting by a sick man's bed, with a crucifix in one hand and with the other in the sufferer's pocket. Things must indeed have been at a low ebb, when the faults of ordained ministers were so publicly held up to scorn.

But the blackest spot on the character of our Pre-Reformation clergy in England is one of which it is painful to speak. I mean the impurity of their lives, and their horrible contempt of the seventh commandment. The results of auricular confession, carried on by men bound by their vow never to marry, were such that I dare not enter into them. The consequences of shutting up herds of men and women, in the prime of life, in monasteries and nunneries, were such that I will not defile my readers' minds by dwelling upon them. Suffice it to say that the discoveries made by Henry VIII's Commissioners, of the state of things in many of the so-called "religious" houses, were such as it is impossible to describe. Anything less "holy" than the practice of many of the "holy" men and women in these professedly "holy" retreats from sin and the world, the imagination cannot conceive! If ever there was a plausible theory weighed in the balance and found utterly wanting, it is the favourite theory that celibacy and monasticism promote holiness. Romantic young men and sentimental young ladies may mourn over the ruins of such Abbeys as Battle, and Glastonbury, and Bolton, and Kirkstall, and Furness, and Croyland, and Bury, and Tintern. But I venture boldly to say that too many of these religious houses were sinks of iniquity, and that too often monks and nuns were the scandal of Christianity.

I grant freely that all monasteries and nunneries were not equally bad. I admit that there were some religious houses like Godstow Nunnery, near Oxford, which had a stainless reputation. But I fear that these were bright exceptions which only prove the truth of the rule. The preamble of the Act for Dissolution of Religious Houses, founded on the report of Henry VIII's Commissioners, contains broad, general statements, that cannot be got over. It declares "that manifest sin, vicious, carnal, and abominable living is daily used and committed in abbeys, priories, and other religious houses of monks, canons, and nuns, and that albeit many continual visitations have been had, by the space of two hundred years and more, for an honest and charitable reformation of such unthrifty, carnal and abominable living, yet that nevertheless little or none amendment was hitherto had, but that their vicious living shamefully increased and augmented."

After all, there is no surer recipe for promoting immorality than "fulness of bread and abundance of idleness." (Ezek. xvi. 49.) Take any number of men and women, of any nation, rank, or class, bind them by a vow of celibacy, shut them up in houses by themselves, give them plenty to eat and drink, and give them nothing to do, and above all, give them no Bible-reading, no true religion, no preaching of the Gospel, no inspection, and no check from public opinion; if the result of all this be not abominable and abundant breach of the seventh commandment, I can only say that I have read human nature in vain.

I make no apology for dwelling on these things. Painful and humbling as the picture is, it is one that in these times ought to be carefully looked at, and not thrown aside. Before we join in the vulgar outcry which some modern Churchmen are making against the Reformation, I want English people to understand from what the Reformation delivered us. Before we make up our minds to give up Protestantism and receive back Popery and monasticism, let us thoroughly understand what was the state of England when Popery had its own way. My own belief is that never was a change so loudly demanded as the Reformation, and that never did men do such good service to England as Hooper and his fellow-labourers, the Reformers. In short, unless a man can disprove the plain historical facts recorded in the pages of Foxe, Fuller, Strype, Burnet, Soames, and Blunt, he must either admit that the Pre-Reformation times were bad times, or be content to be regarded as a lunatic. To no class of men does England owe such a debt as to our Protestant Reformers, and it is a burning shame if we are ungrateful and refuse to pay that debt.

Of course it is easy and cheap work to pick holes in the character of some of the agents whom God was pleased to use at the Reformation. No doubt Henry VIII—who had the Bible translated, and made Cranmer and Latimer bishops, and suppressed the monasteries—was a brutal and bad man. I am not concerned to defend him. But God has often done good work with very bad tools; and the grand result is what we must chiefly look at. And, after all, bad as Henry VIII was, the less our Romanizing friends dwell on that point the better. His moral character at any rate will bear a favourable comparison with that of many of the Popes. At any rate he was a married man!

It is easy, on the other hand, to say that Hooper and his brother Reformers did their work badly, countenanced many abuses, left many things imperfect and incomplete. All this may be very true. But in common fairness men should remember the numerous difficulties they had to contend with, and the mountains of rubbish they had to shovel away. To my mind the wonder is not so much that they did so little, but rather that they succeeded in doing anything at all.

After all, when all has been said, and every objection raised, there remain some great plain facts which cannot well be got over. Let men say what they will, or pick holes where they may, they will never succeed in disproving these facts. To the Reformation Englishmen owe an English Bible, and liberty for every man to read it. To the Reformation they owe the knowledge of the way of peace with God, and of the right of every sinner to go straight to Christ by faith, without bishop, priest, or minister standing in his way. To the Reformation they owe a Scriptural standard of morality and holiness, such as our ancestors never dreamed of. For ever let us be thankful for these inestimable mercies! For ever let us grasp them firmly, and refuse to let them go! For my part, I hold that he who would rob us of these privileges, and draw us back to Pre-Reformation ignorance, superstition, and unholiness, is an enemy to England, and ought to be firmly opposed.

II. I turn from Hooper's times to *Hooper himself*. For dwelling so long on his times I think it needless to make any apology. We cannot rightly estimate a public man, unless we know the times in which he lived. We cannot duly appreciate an English Reformer unless we understand the state of England before the Reformation. We have seen the state of things that Hooper and his companions had to deal with. Now let us find out something about Hooper himself.

John Hooper was born in the county of Somerset, about the year 1495, in the reign of Henry VII. The parish in which he was born is not known, and not even a tradition has survived about it. In this respect Hooper and Rowland Taylor stand alone among the English martyrs. The birthplaces of Cranmer, Ridley, Latimer, Rogers, Bradford, Philpot, and Ferrar have all been ascertained. The position which his family occupied in the county is alike unknown. There is, however, good reason for believing that his father was not a mere yeoman, but a man of considerable wealth.

The early history of this great Reformer is wrapped in much obscurity. He entered Merton College, Oxford, in 1514, under the tuition of an uncle, who was then Fellow of that College. He took the degree of B.A. in 1518, at about the age of twenty-three, and never afterwards proceeded to a higher degree. These are literally the only facts that have been discovered about the first twenty-three years of Hooper's life. From 1518 to 1539, a period of no less than twenty-one years, we are again left almost entirely in the dark about Hooper's history. There can be little doubt, however, that it was a most momentous crisis in his life, and gave a colour and bias to the whole man for the rest of his days. Tradition says, that after taking his degree at Oxford, he became a monk—first at the Cistercian Monastery of Old Cleve, near Watchet, in Somersetshire, and afterwards in another Cistercian house at Gloucester. Tradition adds, that he became wearied and disgusted with a monastic life, and withdrew from it, in order to reside at Oxford; though at what precise date is not known. It is some corroboration of these traditions, that when he was sentenced to death afterwards by Gardiner, he was described as "formerly a monk of the Monastery of Cleve, of the Cistercian order." Yet it must be admitted that there is a conspicuous absence in his literary remains of any reference to his experience as a monk.

One thing, at any rate, is very certain about Hooper at this stage of his life. It was during these twenty-one years, between 1518 and 1539, that his eyes were opened to the false doctrines and unscriptural practices of Popery, though when and where we cannot exactly tell. He says himself, in a letter to Bullinger, the Swiss Reformer, that "when he was a courtier, and living too much of a court life in the palace of our King," he met with certain writings of Zwingli, and certain commentaries of Bullinger on St Paul's Epistles, and that to the study of these books he owed his deliverance from Papacy, and the conversion of his soul. This deeply interesting letter will be found in the "Original Letters from Zurich," published by the Parker Society. To the meaning, however, of the allusion to "a court life," and "the palace of our King," the letter, unfortunately, supplies no clue.

Another fact about Hooper at this period of his history is no less certain. He was obliged to leave Oxford in 1539, when the semi-Popish statute of the Six Articles, which made Latimer resign his Bishopric, was put in operation. Foxe, the Martyrologist, distinctly asserts that his known attachment to the principles of the Reformation attracted the notice of the Oxford authorities, and specially of Dr Smith, the Professor of Divinity. The consequence was, that he was compelled to retire from the University, and appears to have never resided there again.

On leaving Oxford, in 1539, Hooper became, for a short time, steward and chaplain in the household of Sir Thomas Arundel. Here also again his Protestant principles got him into trouble. His master liked him, but did not like his opinions. The consequence was, that he sent him to Bishop Gardiner with a private letter, in which he requested him to "do his chaplain some good." Gardiner, however, after four or five days' conference, could make nothing of the sturdy Reformer, and utterly failed to shake his opinions. The end of the matter, was, says Foxe, "that he sent Sir Thomas his servant again, right well commending his learning and wit, but bearing in his heart a grudge against Master

Hooper." This grudge, unhappily, was not forgotten, and bore bitter fruit after many days.

The connection between Hooper and Sir Thomas Arundel did not last long after this. The Protestant chaplain found that his life was not safe in England, and, like many of the good men of his day, withdrew to the Continent. There he appears to have lived for at least nine years, first at Strasbourg, afterwards at Bâle, and finally at Zurich. It was at this period of his life, no doubt, that he became established in those clear, distinct views of doctrinal truth, which he afterwards so nobly maintained in his own country. At this period, too, he formed friendships with Bullinger, Bucer, à Lasco, and other Continental reformers, who ever afterwards regarded him with deep affection. At this period, too, about the year 1546, he married a noble Burgundian lady, named Anna de Tzerclas, who seems to have been in every way a helpmeet for him.

In 1547 Henry VIII died, and Edward VI commenced his short but glorious reign. Soon after this Hooper began to feel it his bounden duty to give his aid to the work of the Protestant Reformation in his own country, and, after taking an affectionate leave of his Zurich friends, set out on his return to England. His parting words were painfully prophetic and deeply touching. They told him they fully expected that he would rise to a high position in his native land; they hoped he would not forget his old friends; they begged him to write to them sometimes. In reply, Hooper assured them that he should never forget their many kindnesses; promised to write to them from time to time, and concluded with the following memorable words: "The last news of all, Master Bullinger, I shall not be able to write. For there, where I shall take most pains, there shall ye hear of me to be burnt to ashes. That shall be the last news which I shall not be able to write to you. But you shall hear it of me."

Hooper arrived in London in May, 1549, and was gladly received by the friends of the Reformation, which, in the face of immense difficulties, Cranmer and Ridley were slowly pressing forward. He came like a welcome reinforcement in the midst of an arduous campaign, and mightily strengthened the cause of Protestantism. His reputation, as a man of soundness, learning and power, had evidently gone before him. He was very soon appointed chaplain to the Protector, the Duke of Somerset. With characteristic zeal he devoted himself at once to the work of teaching, and generally preached twice a day, and this with such marked acceptance that the churches could not contain the crowds that flocked to hear him. Even Dr Smith, his enemy, confessed that "he was so much admired by the people that they held him for a prophet: nay, they looked upon him as a deity."

Foxe, the Martyrologist, who evidently knew Hooper well, bears the following testimony to his high character at this time, both for gifts and graces: "In his doctrine he was earnest, in tongue eloquent, in the Scriptures perfect, in pains indefatigable. His life was so pure and good that no breath of slander could fasten any fault upon him. He was of body strong, his health whole and sound, his wit very pregnant, his invincible patience able to sustain whatsoever sinister fortune and adversity could do. He was constant of judgment, spare of diet, sparer of words, and sparest of time. In housekeeping he was very liberal, and sometimes more free than his living would extend unto. Briefly, of all those virtues and qualities required of St Paul in a good Bishop, in his Epistle to Timothy, I know not one that was lacking in Master Hooper."

A man of this mould and stamp was rightly esteemed the very man to make a Bishop in Edward VI's days. Within a year of his landing in England the prophecies of his Zurich friends were fulfilled. After preaching a course of Lent sermons before the King in 1550, John Hooper, the friend of Bullinger, the exile of Zurich, the most popular preacher of the day, was nominated to fill the vacant Bishopric of Gloucester. A wiser choice could not have been made. Rarely, too rarely, in the annals of the Church of England has there been such an instance of the right man being put in the right place.

Hooper's nomination, however, brought him into a most unhappy collision with Cranmer and Ridley, on a very awkward subject. He steadily refused to take the oath which had been taken hitherto by Bishops at their consecration, and to wear the episcopal vestments which had hitherto been worn. The oath he objected to as flatly unscriptural, because it referred to the saints as well as God. The vestments he objected to as remnants of Popery, which ought to be clean put away.

A controversy arose at once between Hooper and his two great fellow-labourers, which delayed his consecration almost a whole year, and did immense harm. The more trifling and unimportant the original cause of dispute appeared to be, the more heated and obstinate the disputants became. In vain did Ridley confer and correspond with his recusant brother. In vain did Edward VI and his Privy Council write to Cranmer, and offer to discharge him from all risk of penalties, if he would "let pass certain rites and ceremonies" offensive to the Bishop-designate. In vain did foreign Reformers write long letters, and entreat both parties to concede something and give way. The contention grew so sharp that the Privy Council became weary of Hooper's obstinacy, and actually committed him to the Fleet Prison! At length a compromise was effected. Hooper gave way on some points, for peace' sake. He consented to wear the obnoxious vestments on certain public occasions, at his consecration, before the King, and in his own Cathedral. The objectionable words in the Episcopal Oath were struck out by the King's own hand. The prison gates were then thrown open, and, to the great joy of all true Protestants, Hooper was consecrated Bishop of Gloucester on the 8th of March, 1551.

This miserable controversy between Hooper and his two great opponents, like all the disputes of good men, is a sorrowful subject. Of course it need not surprise us. The best of men are only men at their best. If Paul and Barnabas quarrelled until they parted company, and Peter and Paul came into open collision at Antioch, we must not judge our English Reformers too harshly, if they did not always agree. But it is vain to deny that this famous quarrel did great harm at the time, and sowed seeds which are bearing mischievous fruit down to this very day.

At the distance of more than three hundred years, I freely admit, we are poor judges of the whole case. Both parties undoubtedly were more or less in the wrong, and the only question is as to the side which was most to blame. The general verdict of mankind, I am quite aware, has been against Hooper. To this verdict, however, I must honestly say, I cannot altogether subscribe. It is my deliberate conviction, after carefully weighing the whole affair, that Hooper was most likely in the right, and Cranmer and Ridley were most likely in the wrong.

I believe the plain truth to be, that Hooper was much more far-sighted than his excellent fellow-labourers. He looked further ahead than they did, and saw the possibility of evils arising in the Church of England, of which they in their charity never dreamed. He foresaw, with prophetic eye, the immense peril of leaving nest-eggs for future Romanism within our pale. He foresaw a time when the Pope's friends would take advantage of the least crevice left in the walls of our Zion; and he would fain have had every crack stopped up. He would not have left a single peg on which Romanizing Churchmen could have rehung the abominable doctrine of the Mass. It is my decided opinion that he was quite right. Events have supplied abundant proof that his conscientious scruples were well founded. I believe, if Cranmer and Ridley had calmly listened to his objections, and seized the opportunity of settling the whole question of "vestments" in a thoroughly Protestant way, it would have been a blessing to the Church of England! In a word, if Hooper's views had been allowed to prevail, one half of the Ritualistic controversy of our own day would never have existed at all.[1]

Once delivered from this miserable controversy, Hooper commenced his episcopal duties without a moment's delay. Though only consecrated on the 8th of March, 1551, he began at once to preach throughout the diocese of Gloucester with such a diligence as to cause fears about his health. His wife, writing to Bullinger in the month of April, says, "I entreat you to recommend Master Hooper to be more moderate in his labours. He preaches four, or at least three, times every day, and I am afraid lest these over-abundant exertions should cause a premature decay." Of all the Edwardian Bishops, none seems to have made such full proof of his episcopal ministry as he did. Cranmer was naturally absorbed in working out the great scheme of Reformation, of which he was

[1] It is a pleasing fact, that at a later date there seems to have been a complete reconciliation between Hooper and Ridley, if indeed there ever was a real breach. When Ridley was in prison, in Queen Mary's reign, he wrote as follows to Hooper: "My dear brother, we thoroughly agree and wholly consent together in those things which are the grounds and substantial points of our religion, against which the world so furiously rageth in these days. In time past, by certain by-matters and circumstances of religion, your wisdom and my simplicity hath a little jarred, each of us following the abundance of his own sense and judgment. But now I say, be you assured, that with my whole heart, God is my witness, I love you in the truth, and for the truth's sake!"

the principal architect. Ridley, from his position in London, within reach of the Court and of Lambeth Palace, was necessarily often drawn aside to advise the King and the Primate. For really working a diocese, and giving a splendid pattern of what an English Protestant Bishop should be, the man of the times was John Hooper. We need not wonder that the Government soon gave him the charge of Worcester as well as the diocese of Gloucester. The willing horse is always worked, and the more a man does, the more he is always asked to do.

The state of Hooper's clergy evidently gave him great trouble. We have already seen that many clergymen in the diocese of Gloucester were unable to repeat the Ten Commandments, and could not tell who was the author of the Lord's prayer. Moreover, they were not only ignorant, but generally hostile to the doctrines of the Reformation. However, they were ready to conform to anything, and subscribe anything, so long as they were allowed to keep their livings! Hooper therefore drew up for them a body of fifty Articles of an admirable character, and required every incumbent to subscribe them. He also supplied them with a set of excellent injunctions about their duties. Besides this he appointed some of the better sort to be superintendents of the rest, with a commission to watch over their brethren. It is difficult to see what more he could have done, however painful and unsatisfactory the state of things may have been. The best Bishops, with all their zeal, cannot give grace, or change clerical hearts.

The state of the laity in the diocese of Gloucester was just as unsatisfactory as that of the clergy. This, of course, was only natural. "Like pastors, like people.", With them he could of necessity do little, except reprove immorality, and check it, when possible to do so. Of his firm and impartial conduct in this way, a remarkable example is given by John ab Ulmis, in one of the Zurich letters. He says, that Sir Anthony Kingston, a man of rank in Gloucester, was cited by the Bishop to appear before him, on a charge of adultery, and was severely reprimanded. He replied with abusive language, and even forgot himself so far as to strike Hooper on the cheek. But Hooper was unmoved. He reported the whole case to the Privy Council in London, and the result was that the Gloucestershire Knight was severely punished for his contumacy, and fined no less than £500, a very large sum in those days.

The state of the two Cathedrals of Gloucester and Worcester appears to have been as great a trial to Hooper as the state of the parochial clergy and laity. Curiously enough, even 300 years ago, Cathedral bodies seem to have been anything but helps to the Church of England. He says, in a letter upon this subject to Sir William Cecil, the King's Secretary of State, "Ah! Mr Secretary, that there were good men in the Cathedral churches! God should then have much more honour than He hath, the King's majesty more obedience, and the poor people more knowledge. But the realm wanteth light in such churches where of right it ought most to be." He then concludes his letter with these touching words: "God give us wisdom and strength wisely and strongly to serve in our vocations. There is none that eateth their bread in the sweat of their face but such as serve in public vocation. Yours, Mr Secretary, is wonderful, but mine passeth. Now I perceive private labours be but play, and private troubles but ease and quietness. God be our help!"

After all, the best account of Hooper's discharge of his episcopal duties is to be found in that good old book well known by the title of Foxe's *Martyrs*. Foxe was evidently a friend and admirer of Hooper, and writes about him with a very loving pen. But Foxe may always be depended on for general accuracy. Bitterly as his many enemies have tried to vilify his great book, they have never succeeded in disproving his facts. They may have scratched the good man's face, but they have never broken his bones. Froude, a thoroughly disinterested witness, has voluntarily declared his confidence in Foxe's trustworthiness. Townsend, in a lengthy preface to his excellent and complete edition of the "Acts and Monuments," has answered *seriatim* the attacks of Foxe's enemies.[1] In short, we may rest satisfied that those flippant modern writers who call Foxe "a liar" are only exposing their own ignorance, or their hatred of genuine Protestantism. Let us now hear how Foxe describes Hooper's ways as a Bishop, so long as his episcopate lasted. He says,

"Master Hooper, after all these tumults and vexations sustained

[1] A notable defence of Foxe as a historian of the Reformation period is contained in J. F. Mozley's *John Foxe and his Book* (1940).

about his investing and priestly vestures, at length entering into his diocese, did there employ his time, which the Lord lent him under King Edward's reign, with such diligence as may be a spectacle to all Bishops which shall ever hereafter succeed him, not only in that place, but in whatsoever diocese through the whole realm of England. So careful was he in his cure, that he left neither pains untaken, not ways unsought, how to train up the flock of Christ in the true Word of Salvation, continually labouring in the same. Other men commonly are wont, for lucre or promotion's sake, to aspire to bishoprics, some hunting for them, and some purchasing or buying them, as men used to purchase lordships; and when they have them, are loth to leave them, and thereupon also loth to commit that thing by worldly laws whereby to lose them.

"To this sort of men Master Hooper was clean contrary; who abhorred nothing more than gain, labouring always to save and preserve the souls of his flock. Who, being Bishop of two dioceses, so ruled and guided either of them, and both together, as though he had in charge but one family. No father in his household, no gardener in his garden, no husbandman in his vineyard, was more or better occupied than he in his diocese amongst his flock, going about his towns and villages in teaching and preaching to the people there.

"That time that he had to spare from preaching, he bestowed either in hearing public causes, or else in private study, prayer, and visiting of schools. With his continual doctrine he adjoined due and discreet correction, not so much severe to any as to them which for abundance of riches and wealthy state thought they might do what they listed. And doubtless he spared no kind of people, but was indifferent to all men, as well rich as poor, to the great shame of no small number of men now-a-days. Where many we see so addicted to the pleasing of great and rich men, that in the meantime they have no regard to the meaner sort of poor people, whom Christ hath bought as dearly as the other.

"But now again we will return our talk to Master Hooper, all whose life, in fine, was such, that to the Church and all Churchmen it might be a light and example; to the rest, a perpetual lesson and sermon. Finally, how virtuous and good a Bishop he was, ye may conceive and know evidently by this, that, even as he was hated of none but of them which were evil, so yet the worst of them all could not reprove his life in any one jot.

"I have now declared his usage and behaviour abroad in the public affairs of the Church: and certainly there appeared in him at home no less example of a worthy prelate's life. For though he bestowed and converted the most part of his care upon the public flock and congregation of Christ, for the which also he spent his blood; yet nevertheless there lacked no provision in him to bring up his own children in learning and good manners; insomuch that ye could not discern whether he deserved more praise for his fatherly usage at home, or for his bishop-like doings abroad. For everywhere he kept one religion in one uniform doctrine and integrity. So that if you entered into the Bishop's palace, you would suppose yourself to have entered into some church or temple. In every corner thereof there was some smell of virtue, good example, honest conversation, and reading of holy Scriptures. There was not to be seen in his house any courtly roisting or idleness: no pomp at all, no dishonest word, no swearing could there be heard!

"As for the revenues of both his Bishoprics, although they did not greatly exceed, as the matter was handled, yet if anything surmounted thereof, he pursed nothing, but bestowed it in hospitality. Twice I was, as I remember, in his house in Worcester, where, in his common hall, I saw a table spread with good store of meat, and beset full of beggars and poor folk. And I asking his servants what this meant, they told me that every day their lord and master's manner was to have customably to dinner a certain number of the poor folk of the said city, by course, who were served by four at a mess, with hot and wholesome meats. And when they were served (being before examined by him or his deputies, of the Lord's prayer, the Articles of their faith, and the Ten Commandments), then he himself sat down to dinner, and not before.[1]

"After this sort and manner Master Hooper executed the office of a most careful and vigilant pastor, by the space of two years and more, so long as the state of religion in King Edward's time did safely flourish and take place. And would God that all other

---

[1] It must be remembered that there was no Poor Law in those days.

Bishops would use the like diligence, care, and observance in their function."

III. Hooper's most useful episcopal labours were brought completely to an end by Queen Mary's accession to the throne, in 1553. They did not last, we may observe, much longer than two years. Perhaps it is not too much to say that no Bishop of the Church of England ever did so much for his church and diocese in two years, and left so deep a mark on men's minds in a short period as John Hooper.

Edward VI died in July, 1553; and as soon as his Popish sister Mary was fairly seated on her throne, John Hooper's troubles began. The sword of persecution having been once unsheathed, the famous Protestant Bishop of Gloucester was almost the first person who was struck at. He was personally obnoxious both to Bonner and Gardiner, with both of whom he had come into collision. He was renowned all over England as one of the boldest champions of the Reformation, and most thorough opponents of Popery. His friends warned him that danger was impending, but he calmly replied, "Once I did flee and took me to my feet. But now, because I am called to this place and vocation, I am thoroughly persuaded to tarry, and to live and die with my sheep." The threatening storm soon broke. On the 29th of August he appeared before Queen Mary's Council, at Richmond; and on the 1st of September he was sent as a prisoner to the Fleet. From that day till the 9th February, 1555, a period of more than seventeen months, he was kept in close confinement. On that day, at last, death set him at liberty, and the noble Protestant prisoner was free.

The history of these sorrowful seventeen months in Hooper's life would occupy far more space than I have at my disposal. Those who wish to know the particulars of it must study Foxe's *Martyrs*. How the good Bishop of Gloucester and Worcester was cruelly immured in a filthy prison, to the great injury of his health, for nearly a year and a half, how he was three times examined before such judges as Gardiner, Bonner, Day, Heath, and their companions, how he was by turns insulted, browbeaten, reviled, entreated and begged to recant, how gallantly he stood firm by his Protestant principles, and refused to give up a hair's breadth of Christ's truth, how he was finally condemned for holding the right of priests to marry, and for denying the doctrine of transubstantiation, all these are matters which are fully recorded by the old Martyrologist.

The end came at last. On Monday, the 4th of February, 1555, Hooper was formally degraded by Bishop Bonner, in the chapel of Newgate prison, and handed over to the tender mercies of the secular power. In the evening of that day, to his great delight, he was informed that he was to be sent to Gloucester, and to be publicly burned in his own cathedral city. On Tuesday, the 5th, he commenced his journey on horse-back, at four o'clock in the morning, in the charge of six guards. On the afternoon of Thursday, the 7th of February, he arrived safe at Gloucester, amidst the tears and lamentations of a great crowd of people, who came out to meet him on the Cirencester Road.

At Gloucester he was lodged in the house of one Ingram, opposite to St Nicholas' Church. The house is still standing, and to all appearance not much altered. The city Sheriffs, two men named Jenkins and Bond, would fain have put him in the Northgate prison, but gave up this intention at the earnest intercession of the guards who had brought him from London. One day only was allowed to elapse between the saintly prisoner's arrival and his execution. The greater part of this short interval he spent in prayer. There were, however, some interviews, of no small interest, of which Foxe has preserved a record.

Sir Anthony Kingston, whom he had once offended by rebuking his sins, came to see him, and entreated him, with much affection and many tears, to consult his safety and recant. "Consider," he said, "that life is sweet, and death is bitter. Life hereafter may do good." To this the noble soldier of Christ returned the ever memorable answer: "The life to come is more sweet, and the death to come is more bitter." Seeing him immoveable, Kingston left him with bitter tears, telling him, "I thank God that ever I knew you, seeing God did appoint you to call me, being a lost child. By your good instructions, when I was before a fornicator and adulterer, God hath brought me to detest and forsake the same." Hooper afterwards said that this interview had drawn from him more tears than he had shed throughout the seventeen months of his imprisonment.

Last of all, as evening drew on, the Mayor, Mr Loveday, the

Aldermen, and Sheriffs of Gloucester, came to his lodging, and courteously saluted him. To them he spoke cheerfully, thanking them for their kindness, requesting that there might be a quick fire at his burning, and protesting that he should die a true, obedient subject to the Queen, but "willing to give up his life rather than consent to the wicked papistical religion of the Bishop of Rome."

These interviews got over, the saintly Bishop began to prepare for his wrestle with the last enemy, death. He retired to bed very early, saying that he had many things to remember, and slept one sleep soundly. The rest of the night he spent in prayer. After he got up, he desired that no man should be allowed to come into the chamber, and that he might be left alone till the hour of execution. What his meditations and reflections were at that awful crisis, God alone knows. Tradition says that he wrote the following piece of poetry with a coal, on the wall of his chamber:

> "'Content thyself with patience
>   With Christ to bear the cross of pain:
> Who can or will recompense
>   A thousand-fold, with joys again.
> Let nothing cause thy heart to fail:
> Launch out thy boat, hoist up thy sail,
>   Put from the shore;
> And be thou sure thou shalt attain
> Unto the port, that shall remain
>   For evermore.

> "Fear not death, pass not for bands,
>   Only in God put thy whole trust;
> For He will require thy blood at their hands,
>   And thou dost know that once die thou must,
> Only for that thy life if thou give,
> Death is no death, but amens for to live.
>   Do not despair:
> Of no worldly tyrant be thou in dread;
> Thy compass, which is God's Word, shall thee lead,
>   And the wind is fair."

These lines were printed in 1559, in a volume of miscellaneous pieces by the Reformers. I give them for what they are worth.

The closing scene of Hooper's life had now come. It is so beautifully and simply described by John Foxe, that I think it best to give it in its entirety, with trifling omissions, just as the worthy old Martyrologist wrote it. He says, "On the morning of Saturday, the 9th of February, about eight of the clock, came Sir John Bridges, Lord Chandos, with a great band of men, Sir Anthony Kingston, Sir Edmund Bridges, and other commissioners appointed to see execution done. At nine of the clock, Mr Hooper was willed to prepare himself to be in a readiness, for the time was at hand. Immediately he was brought down from his chamber by the Sheriffs, who were accompanied with bills and weapons. When he saw the multitude of weapons, he spake to the Sheriffs on this wise: 'Mr Sheriffs,' said he, 'I am no traitor, neither needed you to have made such a business to bring me to the place where I must suffer; for if ye had willed me, I would have gone alone to the stake, and have troubled none of you.' Afterward, looking upon the multitude of people that were assembled, being by estimation to the number of 7,000 (for it was market-day, and many also came to see his behaviour towards death), he spake unto those that were about him, saying, 'Alas! why be these people assembled and come together? Peradventure they think to hear something of me now, as they have in times past; but, alas! speech is prohibited me. Notwithstanding, the cause of my death is well known unto them. When I was appointed here to be their pastor, I preached unto them true and sincere doctrine, and that, out of the Word of God. Because I will not now account the same to be heresy and untruth, this kind of death is prepared for me.'

"So he went forward, led between the two Sheriffs (as it were a lamb to the place of slaughter), in a gown of his host's, his hat upon his head, and a staff in his hand to stay himself withal; for the grief of the sciatica, which he had taken in prison, caused him somewhat to halt. All the way, being strictly charged not to speak, he could not be perceived once to open his mouth; but beholding the people all the way, which mourned bitterly for him, he would sometimes lift up his eyes towards heaven, and looked very cheerfully upon such as he knew; and he was never known, during the time of his being amongst them to look with so cheerful and ruddy a countenance as he did at that present. When he came to the place appointed where he should die, smilingly he beheld the stake and preparation made for him, which was near unto the great elm-tree over against the college of priests, where he was wont to preach. The place round about the houses, and the boughs of the trees, were replenished with people: and in the chamber over the college gate stood the priests of the college.[1] Then kneeled he down (forasmuch as he could not be suffered to speak unto the people) to prayer, and beckoned six or seven times unto one whom he knew well, to hear the said prayer, to make report thereof in time to come who (pouring tears upon his shoulders and in his bosom) gave attentive ear unto the same; the which prayer he made upon the whole Creed, wherein he continued the space of half-an-hour. Now, after he was somewhat entered into his prayer, a box was brought and laid before him upon a stool, with his pardon (or at leastwise, it was feigned to be his pardon) from the Queen, if he would turn. At the sight whereof he cried, 'If you love my soul, away with it! If you love my soul, away with it!' The box being taken away, the Lord Chandos said, 'Seeing there is no remedy, dispatch him quickly!' Master Hooper said, 'Good my lord: I trust your lordship will give me leave to make an end of my prayers.'

"Then said the Lord Chandos to Sir Edmund Bridges' son, which gave ear before to Master Hooper's prayer, at his request: 'Edmund, take heed that he do nothing else but pray; if he do, tell me, and I shall quickly dispatch him.' While this talk was going on, there stepped one or two in uncalled, which heard him speak these words following:

" 'Lord,' said he, 'I am hell, but Thou art heaven; I am swill and a sink of sin, but Thou art a gracious God and a merciful Redeemer. Have mercy, therefore, upon me, most miserable and wretched offender, after Thy great mercy, and according to Thine inestimable goodness. Thou that art ascended into heaven, receive me, hell, to be partaker of Thy joys, where Thou sittest in equal glory with Thy Father. For well knowest Thou, Lord, wherefore I am come hither to suffer, and why the wicked do persecute this Thy poor servant: not for my sins and transgressions committed

[1] This gateway and the window are still standing exactly as they were when Hooper was burned.

against Thee, but because I will not allow their wicked doings to the contaminating of Thy blood, and to the denial of the knowledge of Thy truth, wherewith it did please Thee by Thy Holy Spirit to instruct me; the which with as much diligence as a poor wretch might (being thereto called), I have set forth to Thy glory. And well seest Thou, my Lord and God, what terrible pains and cruel torments be prepared for Thy creature; such, Lord, as without Thy strength none is able to bear, or patiently to pass. But all things that are impossible with man are possible with Thee. Therefore, strengthen me of Thy goodness, that in the fire I break not the rules of patience; or else assuage the terror of the pains, as shall seem most to Thy Glory.'

"As soon as the Mayor had espied these men which made report of the former words, they were commanded away, and could not be suffered to hear any more. Prayer being done, he prepared himself to the stake, and put off his host's gown, and delivered it to the Sheriffs, requiring them to see it restored unto the owner, and put off the rest of his gear, unto his doublet and hose, wherein he would have been burned. But the Sheriffs would not permit that (such was their greediness),[1] unto whose pleasures (good man) he very obediently submitted himself; and his doublet, hose, and waistcoat were taken off. Then, being in his shirt, and desiring the people to say the Lord's Prayer with him, and to pray for him, (who performed it with tears, during the time of his pains,) he went up to the stake. Now, when he was at the stake, three irons, made to bind him to the stake, were brought: one for his neck, another for his middle, and the third for his legs. But he, refusing them, said, 'Ye have no need thus to trouble yourselves, for I doubt not but God will give me strength sufficient to abide the extremity of the fire, without bands; notwithstanding, suspecting the frailty and weakness of the flesh, but having assured confidence in God's strength, I am content ye do as ye shall think good.' So the hoop of iron prepared for his middle was brought, and when they offered to have bound his neck and legs with the other two hoops of iron, he utterly refused them, and would have none, saying, 'I am well assured I shall not trouble you.'

"Thus, being ready, he looked upon the people, of whom he

[1] The clothes of those who were burned seemed to have been the perquisite of the Sheriffs.

might well be seen (for he was both tall and stood also on an high stool), and beheld round about him: and in every corner there was nothing to be seen but weeping and sorrowful people. Then, lifting up his eyes and hands unto heaven, he prayed to himself. By and by, he that was appointed to make the fire came to him, and did ask his forgiveness. Of whom he asked why he should forgive him; saying, that he knew never any offence he had committed against him. 'O sir,' said the man, 'I am appointed to make the fire.' 'Therein,' said Mr Hooper, 'thou dost nothing offend me: God forgive thee thy sins, and do thine office, I pray thee.' Then the reeds were cast up, and he received two bundles of them in his own hands, embraced them, kissed them, and put under either arm one of them, and showed with his hand how the rest should be bestowed, and pointed to the place where any did lack.

"Anon commandment was given that the fire should be set to, and so it was. But because there were put to no fewer green faggots than two horses could carry upon their backs, it kindled not by and by, and was a pretty while also before it took the reeds upon the faggots. At length it burned about him, but the wind having full strength in that place (it was a lowering and cold morning), it blew the flame from him, so that he was in a manner no more but touched by the fire.

"Within a space after, a few dry faggots were brought, and a new fire kindled with faggots (for there were no more reeds), and that burned at his nether parts, but had small power above, because of the wind, saving that it did burn his hair, and scorch his skin a little. In the time of which fire, even as at the first flame, he prayed, saying mildly, and not very loud (but as one without pains), 'O Jesus, the Son of David, have mercy upon me, and receive my soul!' After the second fire was spent, he did wipe both his eyes with his hands, and beholding the people, he said with an indifferent loud voice, 'For God's love, good people, let me have more fire!' And all this while his nether parts did burn, for the faggots were so few that the flame did not burn strongly at his upper parts.

"The third fire was kindled within a while after, which was more extreme than the other two; and then the bladders of gunpowder brake, which did him small good, they were so placed, and the wind had such power. In the which fire he prayed with somewhat a loud voice, 'Lord Jesus, have mercy upon me! Lord Jesus, have mercy upon me! Lord Jesus, receive my spirit!' And these were the last words he was heard to utter. But when he was black in the mouth, and his tongue swollen that he could not speak, yet his lips went till they were shrunk to the gums; and he knocked his breast with his hands until one of his arms fell off, and then knocked still with the other, what time the fat, water, and blood dropped out at his fingers' ends, until by renewing of the fire his strength was gone, and his hand did cleave fast in knocking to the iron upon his breast. So immediately, bowing forwards, he yielded up his spirit.

"Thus was he three quarters of an hour or more in the fire. Even as a lamb, patiently he abode the extremity thereof, neither moving forwards, backwards, nor to any side; but having his nether parts burned, and his bowels fallen out, he died as quietly as a child in his bed, and he now reigneth as a blessed martyr in the joys of heaven, prepared for the faithful in Christ before the foundations of the world, for whose constancy all Christians are bound to praise God."[1] (Foxe's "Acts and Monuments" *in loco.*)

I leave the story of the martyr of Gloucester at this point, having traced his life from his cradle to his fiery grave. He died as he had long lived, true to his colours; and his death was every way worthy of his life.

Something I might say about the hideous cruelty with which he and his fellow-sufferers in Mary's reign were put to death. Nothing can excuse it. The times, no doubt, were rough and coarse. Capital punishment was fearfully common. Killing people for alleged heresy was unhappily no strange thing. But these are poor defences of a huge crime. The blood of the English martyrs is an undelible stain on the Church of Rome. It was a judicial murder that can never be explained away.

[1] The stump of a very large oaken post, blackened and charred with fire, was dug up a few years ago on the very place where Hooper was burned. It is supposed by many to be the lower end of the stake to which the martyr was chained when he met his fiery death. Of course no positive proof can be given that this supposition is correct; but there is no improbability or impossibility in the idea. A well-seasoned charred piece of oak timber might easily last undecayed in the ground for three centuries. I saw this stump with my own eyes under a glass case, in a house near Gloucester, where it was carefully preserved.

Something I might say about the glorious patience and courage which Hooper exhibited throughout his sufferings. As long as the world lasts, he will be a pattern of what Christ can do for His people in the hour of need. Never may we forget that He who strengthened Hooper never changes. He is "the same yesterday, and to-day, and for ever."

Something, not least, I might say about the extreme impolicy of the Church of Rome in making martyrs of Hooper and his companions. Never, I believe, did Popery do herself such damage as when she burnt our Reformers. Their blood was the seed of the Church. The good that they did by their deaths was more than they did all their lives. Their martyrdoms made thousands think who were never reached by their sermons. Myriads, we may depend, came to the conclusion that a Church which could act so abominably and cruelly as Rome did could never be the one true Church of God; and that a cause which could produce such patient and unflinching sufferers must surely be the cause of Christ and of truth.

But I pass away from these points, however interesting. I only hope that they may be seeds of thought which may bear fruit in men's minds after many days.

IV. The last point which I wish to bring under the notice of my readers is one which I feel to be of deep importance. I have supplied some information about Hooper's life and death. I will now ask my readers to give me their attention a little longer, while I say something about Hooper's *opinions*. I have shown you how he lived and died, let me now show you exactly what he thought, and what he taught, and what he preached. I have set before you the man, let me now set before you his doctrine.

If I left my readers under the vague impression that Hooper was a good man and a zealous man and an earnest man, but told them nothing more, I should think I had not done my duty. I want men to understand what theological views the martyred Bishop of Gloucester held. I want men to see clearly what kind of doctrine was taught by the English Reformers. What kind of things did Hooper say, and preach, and publish, and write? What kind of religion was a Churchman's religion at the Reformation?

The answer to these inquiries is happily not difficult to find.

The two volumes of Hooper's writings published by the Parker Society, make the matter plain as the sun at noon-day. There men may read in unmistakable language the theological opinions of one of the leading Bishops of the time of the Reformation. From two documents in these two volumes I will select fair specimens.

The first document I will quote from is entitled "Articles concerning the Christian religion, given by the reverend father in Christ, John Hooper, Bishop of Gloucester, unto all and singular deans, parsons, prebends, vicars, curates, and other ecclesiastical ministers within the diocese of Gloucester, to be had, and retained of them for unity and agreement, as well for the doctrine of God's Word, as also for the conformity of the ceremonies agreeing with God's Word."

A more authoritative and weighty declaration of Hooper's opinions, it is impossible to conceive.[1]

The *First Article* enjoins, "that none of the above-named clergy do diligently teach and preach any manner of thing to be necessary for the salvation of men, other than that which is contained in the Book of God's Holy Word, called the Old and New Testament; and that they beware to establish and confirm any manner of doctrine concerning the old superstitious and papistical doctrines, which cannot be duly and justly approved by the authority of God's Word.'

The *Fourth Article* enjoins, "that they and every one of them do diligently teach and preach that the Church of God is the congregation of the faithful, wherein the Word of God is truly preached, and the Sacraments justly administered according to the institution of Christ, and His doctrine taught unto us by His Holy Word; and that the Church of God is not by God's Word taken for the multitude or company of men, as of bishops, priests, and such other; but that it is the company of all men hearing God's Word and obeying the same, lest any man should be seduced, believing himself to be bound to any ordinary succession of bishops and priests, but only to the Word of God and the right use of the Sacraments."

The *Seventh Article* enjoins, "that they and every one of them do diligently teach and preach the justification of man to come only

[1] It is worth noticing, that Ridley published many of the same Articles about the same time, for the clergy of the Diocese of London.

by faith of Jesus Christ, and not by the merit of any man's good works, albeit that good works do necessarily follow justification, the which before justification are of no value or estimation before God."

In the *Ninth Article*, he enjoins them, "that the doctrine of purgatory, pardons, prayer for them that are departed out of this world, the veneration, invocation, and worshipping of saints or images, is contrary and injurious to the honour of Christ, our only Mediator and Redeemer, and also against the doctrine of the first and second commandments of God."

In the *Tenth Article*, he enjoins, "that in the Sacrament of the body and blood of the Lord there is no transubstantiation of the bread and wine into the body and blood of Christ, or any manner of corporal or local presence of Christ, in, under, or with the bread and wine, but spiritually, by faith."

In the *Eleventh Article*, he enjoins, "that they which do unworthily come to baptism or the Supper of the Lord, do not receive the virtue and true effect of the same Sacraments, although they receive the external signs and elements."

In the *Twenty-fourth Article*, he enjoins, "that the Sacraments are not of any force by virtue or strength of any outward work of the same, which of superstition is called *opus operatum*, but only by the virtue and means of the Holy Ghost working in the hearts of the doers and receivers by faith."

In the *Forty-first Article*, he enjoins, "that none of you do counterfeit the Popish Mass, by blessing the Lord's board, washing your hands or fingers after the Gospel, or receipt of the Holy Communion, shifting the Book from one place to another, laying down and licking the chalice after the Communion, showing the Sacrament openly before the distribution of the same, or making any elevation thereof, ringing of the sacring bell, or setting any light on the Lord's board."

In the *Forty-third Article*, he enjoins, "Whereas in divers places some use the Lord's board after the form of a table, and some of an altar, whereby dissension is perceived to arise among the unlearned, therefore, wishing a godly unity to be observed in all our diocese, and for that the form of a table may more move, and turn the simple from the old superstitious opinions of the Popish Mass, and to the right use of the Lord's Supper, we exhort you to erect and set up the Lord's board after the form of an honest table, decently covered, in such place as shall be thought most meet, so that the ministers and communicants may be seen, heard, and understood of all the people there present, and that ye do take down and abolish all altars. Further, that the minister, in the use of the Communion and prayers thereof, turn his face towards the people."

Such were the visitation articles and injunctions of a Bishop of the time of the Reformation. I turn away from them with one single remark. There have been many dioceses in England in the last 300 years in which it might have done great good if the injunctions of good Bishop Hooper had been distributed among the clergy, and urged on their attention.

The only other document that I shall quote from is called "A Brief and Clear Confession of the Christian Faith." It deserves special attention, because it was published in 1550, the very year in which the writer was nominated Bishop of Gloucester. From the "Confession of Faith" I now make the following selections. I make them with considerable difficulty. The whole Confession is so good that it is hard to say what to quote and what to leave behind. I only ask my readers to remember that the sack is as good as the sample.

In the *Twenty-sixth Article* of the Confession, Hooper says, "I do believe and confess that Christ's condemnation is mine absolution; that His crucifying is my deliverance; His descending into hell is mine ascending into heaven; His death is my life; His blood is my cleansing, and purging, by whom only I am washed, purified, and cleansed from all my sins: so that I neither receive, neither believe any other purgatory, either in this world or in the other, whereby I may be purged, but only the blood of Jesus Christ, by which all are purged and made clean for ever."

In the *Twenty-eighth Article* of the Confession, Hooper says, "I believe that the Holy Supper of the Lord is not a sacrifice, but only a remembrance and commemoration of this holy sacrifice of Jesus Christ. Therefore it ought not to be worshipped as God, neither as Christ therein contained; who must be worshipped in faith only, without all corruptible elements. Likewise I believe and confess that the Popish Mass is the invention and ordinance of man, a sacrifice of Antichrist, and a forsaking of the sacrifice of

Jesus Christ, that is to say, of His death and passion; and that it is a stinking and infected sepulchre, which hideth and covereth the merit of the blood of Christ, and, therefore, ought the Mass to be abolished, and the Holy Supper of the Lord to be restored and set in his perfection again."

In the *Fifty-fourth Article* of the Confession, Hooper says, "I believe that the Word of God is of a far greater authority than the Church; the which Word only doth sufficiently show and teach us all those things that in any wise concern our salvation, both what we ought to do and what to leave undone. The same Word of God is the true pattern and perfect rule, after the which all faithful people ought to govern and order their lives, without turning either to the right hand or to the left hand, without changing anything thereof, without putting to it, or taking from it, knowing that all the works of God are perfect, but most chiefly His Word."

In the *Sixty-fourth Article* of the Confession, Hooper says, "I believe that in the holy Sacrament the signs, or badges, are not changed in any point, but the same do remain wholly in their nature; that is to say, the bread is not changed and transubstantiated (as the fond Papists, and false doctors do teach, deceiving the poor people), into the body of Jesus Christ, neither is the wine transubstantiated into His blood; but the bread remaineth still bread, and the wine remaineth still wine, everyone in his proper and first nature."

In the *Sixty-fifth Article* of the Confession, Hooper says, "I believe that all this sacrament consisteth in the use thereof; so that without the right use the bread and wine in nothing differ from other common bread and wine that is commonly used: and, therefore I do not believe that the body of Christ can be contained, hid, or enclosed in the bread, under the bread, or with the bread; neither the blood in the wine, under the wine, or with the wine. But I believe and confess the very body of Christ to be in heaven, on the right hand of the Father (as before we have said), and that always and as often as we use this bread and wine according to the ordinance and institution of Christ, we do verily and indeed receive His body and blood."

In the *Sixty-sixth Article* of the Confession, Hooper says, "I believe that this receiving is not done carnally or bodily, but spiritually, through a true and lively faith; that is to say, the body and blood of Christ are not given to the mouth and belly for the nourishing of the body, but unto our faith for the nourishing of the spirit and inward man unto eternal life. And for that cause we have no need that Christ should come from heaven to us, but that we should ascend unto Him, lifting up our hearts through a lively faith on high unto the right hand of the Father, where Christ sitteth, from whence we wait for our redemption; and we must not seek for Christ in these bodily elements."

I drop my quotations here. I have given enough to make it clear what kind of opinions Hooper held, and what his theological views were. I know not what my readers may think of these quotations. But I will tell you what impression they leave on my mind.

They supply plain proof, for which I am deeply thankful, that Protestant and Evangelical Churchmen are not men of newfangled and modern opinions, but Churchmen of the stamp of the Reformation, Churchmen whose views were held by an eminent Churchman three hundred years ago. Let them take courage. Let them not be moved by the sneers, and taunts, and hard words of those Churchmen who do not agree with them. They may boldly reply that theirs are the old paths, and that they are the true representatives of the Church of England. If Evangelical Churchmen are wrong, then Hooper was wrong too. If Hooper was right, then they are right. But as for a material difference between their views and those of the martyred Bishop of Gloucester, I defy any one to show that there is any at all.

My task is done. I have brought together as concisely as possible the times, life, death, and opinions of one of our greatest English Reformers. But I cannot leave of without offering two practical suggestions to all into whose hands this paper may fall. I address them to each reader personally and directly, and I entreat him to ponder well what I say.

(1) For one thing, I charge all loyal Churchmen to *resist manfully the efforts now being made to unprotestantize England*, and to bring her once more into subjection to Popery. Let us not go back to ignorance, superstition, priestcraft, and immorality. Our forefathers tried Popery long ago, and threw it off with disgust and indignation. Let us not put the clock back and return to Egypt.

Let us have no peace with Rome, till Rome abjures her errors and is at peace with Christ.

Let us read *our Bibles*, and be armed with Scriptural arguments. A Bible-reading laity is a nation's surest defence against error. I have no fear for English Protestantism, if the laity will only do their duty.

Let us read *history*, and see what Rome did in days gone by. Read how she trampled on your country's liberties, plundered your forefather's pockets, and kept the whole nation ignorant and immoral. Read Foxe, and Strype, and Burnet, and Soames, and Blunt. And do not forget that Rome never changes. It is her boast and glory that she is always the same. Only give her absolute power in England, and she would soon put out the eyes of our country, and make her like Samson, a degraded slave.

Let us read *facts* standing out on the face of the globe. What has made Italy what she is? Popery. What has made Mexico and the South American States what they are? Popery. What has made Spain and Portugal what they are? Popery. What has made Ireland what she is? Popery. What makes Scotland, the United States, and our own beloved England, the powerful, prosperous countries that they are at present, and I pray God they may long continue? I answer in one word, Protestantism, a free Bible and a Protestant ministry, and the principles of the Reformation. Let us think twice before we give ear to the specious arguments of liberalism falsely so called. Let us think twice before we help to bring back the reign of Popery.

(2) For another thing, I charge all loyal churchmen, and all who love pure Evangelical religion *to stand together in these days of division, and not allow crotchets and scruples to keep them asunder*. Let the friend of Liturgical Revision drop his favourite panacea for a little space, and put his shoulder to the work of maintaining the Gospel in the Church of England. Let the friend of revivals not think it mis-spent time to give his aid in opposing Rome. If Popery once triumph, there will be no more liberty for revivals. We cannot afford to lose friends. Our ranks are already very thin. The Church of England demands of every Protestant and Evangelical Churchman, that he will do his duty.

Things look black in every direction, I freely admit. But there is no cause to despair. The day is not lost. There is yet time to win a battle. Come what will, let us not desert our position, or forsake the good old ship yet. Let us not please our enemies by spiking our guns, and marching out of our fortress without a battle. Rather let us stand to our guns, like good Bishop Hooper, and in God's strength show a bold front to the foe. The Church of England has done some good in days gone by, and the Church is still worth preserving. If we do go down in the struggle, let us go down with colours flying. But let us stand firm, like the gallant sentinel of Pompeii; let no man leave his post. My own mind is fully made up. I say the Church of England had better perish and go to pieces than forsake John Hooper's principles and tolerate the sacrifice of the Mass, and auricular confession.

NOTE

THE FOLLOWING LETTER IS WELL WORTH READING

"A Letter which Master Hooper did write out of Prison to certain of his Friends, three weeks before his cruel Burning at Gloucester.

"The grace of God be with you. Amen.

"I did write unto you of late, and told you what extremity the Parliament had concluded upon concerning religion, suppressing the truth, and setting forth the untrue, intending to cause all men by extremity to forswear themselves, and to take again for the head of the Church him that is neither head nor member of it, but a very enemy, as the Word of God and all ancient writers do record: and for lack of law and authority, they will use force and extremity, which have been the arguments to defend the Pope and Popery since this wicked authority first began in the world. But now is the time of trial, to see whether we fear more God or man. It was an easy thing to hold with Christ while the Prince and world held with Him; but now the world hateth Him, is the true trial who be His. Wherefore, in the name and in the virtue, strength, and power of His Holy Spirit, prepare yourselves in any case to adversity and constancy. Let us not run away when it is most time to fight. Remember, none shall be crowned but such as fight manfully; and *he that endureth to the end shall be saved.* You must now turn all your cogitations from the peril you see, and mark by faith what followeth the peril, either victory in this world of your enemies, or else a surrender of this life to inherit the everlasting kingdom. Beware of beholding too much the felicity or misery of this world; for the consideration and earnest love or fear of either of them draweth from God. Wherefore think with yourselves, as touching the felicity of the world, it is good; but yet none otherwise than it standeth with the favour of God. It is to be kept; but yet so far forth, as by keeping of it we lose not God. It is good abiding and tarrying still among our friends here; but yet so, that we tarry not therewithal in God's displeasure, and hereafter dwell in hell with the devils in fire everlasting. There is nothing under God but may be kept, so that God, being above all things we have, be not lost.

"Of adversity judge the same. Imprisonment is painful; but yet liberty upon evil conditions is more painful. The prisons stink, but yet not so much as sweet houses where the fear and true honour of God lacketh. I must be alone and solitary; it is better so to be, and have God with me, than to be in company with the wicked. Loss of goods is great; but loss of God's grace and favour is greater. . . . It is better to make answer before the pomp and pride of wicked men than to stand naked in the sight of all heaven and earth before the just God at the latter day. I shall die by the hands of the cruel man: he is blessed that loseth this life, full of mortal miseries, and findeth the life full of eternal joys. It is pain and grief to depart from goods and friends, but yet not so much as to depart from grace and heaven itself. Wherefore there is neither felicity nor adversity of this world that can appear to be great, if it be weighed with the joys or pains in the world to come.

"I can do no more but pray for you; do the same for me, for God's sake. For my part (I thank the heavenly Father), I have made mine accounts, and appointed myself unto the will of the heavenly Father; as He will, so I will, by His grace. For God's sake, as soon as ye can, send my poor wife and children some letter from you; and my letter also, which I sent of late to D. As it is told me, she never had letter from me, since the coming of Master S. unto her; the more to blame the messengers, for I have written divers times. The Lord comfort them, and provide for them; for I am able to do nothing in worldly things. She is a godly and wise woman. If my meaning had been accomplished, she should have had necessary things; but what I meant God can perform, to whom I commend both her and you all. I am a precious jewel now, and daintily kept, never so daintily; for neither mine own man, nor any of the servants of the house, may come to me, but my keeper alone, a simple, rude man, God knoweth but I am nothing careful thereof. Fare you well. The 21st of January, 1555.

"Your bounden,

"JOHN HOOPER."

ROWLAND TAYLOR: MARTYR

Rowland Taylor, Rector of Hadleigh, in Suffolk, one of the famous Protestant martyrs in Queen Mary's days, is a man about whom the Church possesses singularly little information. Excepting the facts related by John Foxe in the "Book of Martyrs," we know scarcely anything about him. Enough, however, is on record to show that among the noble champions of Christ's truth, who sealed their faith with their blood at the time of the English Reformation, Rowland Taylor was second to none.

The causes of this absence of information are easily explained. For one thing, the good man lived, and laboured, and died, in a small country town, fifty miles from London. Such a position is fatal to a world-wide celebrity. It is the dwellers in large cities, and the occupiers of metropolitan pulpits, whose doings are chronicled by admirers, and whose lives are carefully handed down to posterity. For another thing, he wrote no books, either expository, or controversial, or practical. Not even a single sermon of the martyred Rector of Hadleigh exists in print, and enables him though dead, to speak. When he died, he left nothing behind him to keep his memory alive in libraries. These two facts must not be forgotten.

The account of Taylor, which Foxe has supplied, is so peculiarly graphic and vivid, that one might almost suppose that the Martyrologist was a personal friend of the martyr, or an eye-witness of his sufferings. Of this, however, I can find no evidence. Yet it is worthy of notice, that Foxe, after Queen Elizabeth came to the throne, resided for a considerable time with Parkhurst, Bishop of Norwich, in whose diocese Hadleigh was then situated. He also seems to have had friends and acquaintances at Ipswich, which is only ten miles from Hadleigh. It is therefore highly probable that he had frequent opportunities of visiting Taylor's parish, and very likely received much information from people who were actually present when the noble martyr was burned, and could supply full and accurate accounts both of his ministry and his sufferings. To condense and modernize Foxe's narrative, and to present it to my readers in a convenient form, is the simple object of these pages.

Rowland Taylor, according to Strype, was born at Rothbury, in Northumberland; the same county, it may be remembered, from which Bishop Ridley came. The date of his birth, the rank or position of his family, his early history, and the place of his education, are all things about which nothing whatever is known. We only gather from various sources, that in due time he became a student at Cambridge, and there imbibed the principles of the Protestant Reformation. Among other means by which he was influenced at this important crisis of his life, the sermons of Bishop Latimer are especially named. The first distinct fact in his life that we know is his intimacy with Archbishop Cranmer. In that great man's household he seems to have occupied some office, and to have worked with him in carrying forward the mighty building of the English Reformation. How long he lived with Cranmer, we have, unfortunately, no means of finding out. But there is strong internal evidence that he was so long and so intimately connected with him, that he became a marked man among the English Reformers. Upon no other supposition can we explain the peculiar enmity with which he was sought out and persecuted to death in Queen Mary's reign. The old parson of Hadleigh must surely have obtained an honourable reputation in London, in the days of Edward VI.

Hadleigh, in Suffolk, was the first and only piece of preferment which we know of Rowland Taylor holding. To this he was appointed by his friend Archbishop Cranmer, but at what date we have no means of ascertaining. One thing only is quite certain: as soon as he was appointed to Hadleigh, he resigned all his offices in London, and devoted himself entirely to the work of his parish.

Hadleigh is a small town on the south-west border of Suffolk, containing at the present time, about 4,000 people. The character of the place in the days of Edward VI, and the nature of Rowland Taylor's ministry, are so well and graphically described by Foxe in "Acts and Monuments," that I cannot do better than quote his words:

"The town of Hadleigh was one of the first that received the Word of God in all England, at the preaching of Master Thomas Bilney, by whose industry the Gospel of Christ had such gracious success, and took such root there, that a great number in that parish became exceeding well learned in the Holy Scriptures, as well women as men; so that a man might have found among them many that had often read the whole Bible through, and that could have said a great part of St Paul's Epistles by heart, and very well and readily have given a godly learned sentence in any matter of controversy.

"Their children and servants were also brought up and trained diligently in the right knowledge of God's Word, so that the whole town seemed rather a university of the learned, than a town of cloth-making or labouring people; and what most is to be commended, they were for the most part followers of God's Word in their living.

"In this town of Hadleigh, Dr Taylor was a good shepherd, abiding and dwelling among his sheep. He gave himself wholly to the study of Holy Scripture, most faithfully endeavouring himself to fulfil that charge which the Lord gave unto Peter, saying, 'Peter, lovest thou Me? Feed my lambs,' 'Feed my sheep,' 'Feed my sheep.' This love of Christ so wrought in him, that no Sunday nor holy day passed, nor other time, when he might get the people together, but he preached to them the Word of God, the doctrine of their salvation.

"Not only was his word a preaching unto them, but all his life and conversation was an example of unfeigned Christian life and true holiness. He was void of all pride, humble and meek as any child; so that none were so poor but they might boldly, as unto their father, resort unto him. Neither was his lowliness childish or fearful; but as occasion, time, and place required, he would be stout in rebuking the sinful and evil doers: so that none was so rich but he would tell him plainly his fault, with such earnest and grave rebukes as became a good curate and pastor. He was a man very mild, void of all rancour, grudge, or evil will, ready to do good to all men, readily forgiving his enemies, and never sought to do evil to any.

"To the poor that were blind, sick, lame, bedridden, or that had many children, he was a very father, a careful patron, a diligent provider, insomuch that he caused the parishioners to make a general provision for them; and he himself (beside the continual relief that they always found at his house) gave an honest portion yearly to the common alms box.

"His wife, also, was an honest, discreet, and sober matron; and his children well nurtured, brought up in the fear of God and good learning.

'To conclude, he was a right and lively image or pattern of all those virtuous qualities described by St Paul in a true bishop, a good salt of the earth, savourly, biting the corrupt manners of evil men; a light in God's house set upon a candlestick, for all good men to imitate and follow."

How long Taylor's ministry lasted at Hadleigh we do not exactly know. Foxe only says that he continued there "all the days of the most innocent and holy King of blessed memory, King Edward VI." We may, however, safely conclude that he was there more than ten years. When he was put in prison in Queen Mary's days, he was the father of nine children; and as it is not probable that he would marry until he left Cranmer's household and had a home of his own, it seems likely that his children were all born at Hadleigh. All this, however, is only a matter of conjecture. Enough for us to know that he was evidently Rector of Hadleigh long enough to be loved and honoured by the mass of his parishioners.

Rowland Taylor's quiet days at Hadleigh were soon brought to an end when Queen Mary came to the throne. A man of his eminence and high reputation as a Protestant was sure to be marked for destruction by the Popish party, and an excuse was soon found for putting him in prison.

In the best worked parishes, and under the most faithful preaching of the Gospel, there will always be found many who hate vital religion, and remain hardened, impenitent, and unbelieving. It was so in the days of the Apostles. It is so at the present time in our own parishes. It was so at Hadleigh, when Rowland Taylor was Rector. There were men who hated him, because his doctrine condemned their own lives and opinions; and as soon as they had an opportunity of doing him an injury, they eagerly seized it. Two of these men, named Foster and Clerk, conspired to bring the worthy Rector into collision with the higher powers, by hiring one John Averth, Rector of Aldham, to come to Hadleigh church and celebrate the Popish Mass. The result answered their expectations. Rowland Taylor, with righteous indignation, rushed into the church as the Mass was about to begin, and protested warmly against the whole proceeding, as illegal and idolatrous. Then followed an unseemly altercation, the forcible expulsion of the Rector of Hadleigh from his own church, great excitement among the faithful parishioners, throwing of stones into the church, and a general ferment among the people. All this was duly reported to Stephen Gardiner, Bishop of Winchester and Lord Chancellor of England; and the upshot of the affair, as the malignants had foreseen, was a summons from Gardiner to Dr Taylor, to appear before him in London without delay. This summons the gallant Reformer promptly obeyed, and left Hadleigh, never to return till the day of his death.

When the summons arrived, Rowland Taylor's many friends tried in vain to persuade him to fly to the Continent to save his life, as many other faithful Protestants had done. But they had no more effect on the good old man than Paul's friends had on the Apostle, when they entreated him not to go up to Jerusalem. This was his reply: "What will ye have me to do? I am now old, and have already lived too long, to see these terrible and most wicked days. Fly you, and do as your conscience leadeth you. I am fully determined, with God's grace, to go to the Bishop, and to tell him to his beard that he doth naught. God shall well hereafter raise up teachers of His people, which shall, with much more diligence and fruit, teach them than I have done. For God will not forsake His Church, though now for a time He trieth and correcteth us, and not without just cause.

"As for me, I believe before God I shall never be able to do God so good a service as I may do now, nor shall I ever have so glorious a calling as I have now, nor so great mercy of God proffered me, as is now at this present. For what Christian man would not gladly die against the Pope and his adherents? I know that the Papacy is the kingdom of Antichrist, altogether full of falsehoods; so that all their doctrine is nothing but idolatry, superstition, error, hypocrisy, and lies.

'Wherefore I beseech you and all my other friends to pray for me, and I doubt not but God will give me strength and His Holy Spirit, that all mine adversaries shall have shame of their doings."

Armed with this frame of mind, Rowland Taylor went voluntarily to London, and most manfully kept his word. The opening of his first interview with Gardiner is thus described by Foxe:

"Now when Gardiner saw Dr Taylor, according to his common custom, he reviled him, calling him knave, traitor, heretic, with many other villainous reproaches. All this Dr Taylor heard patiently, and at last said, 'My lord, I am neither traitor nor heretic, but a true subject, and a faithful Christian man; and I am come according to your commandment, to know what is the cause why your lordship hath sent for me.'

"Then said the Bishop, 'Art thou come, thou villain? How darest thou look me in the face for shame? Knowest thou not who I am?'

" 'Yes!' said Dr Taylor, 'I know who you are: you are Dr Stephen Gardiner, Bishop of Winchester and Lord Chancellor, and yet but a mortal man. If I should be afraid of your lordly looks, why fear you not God, the Lord of us all? How dare you for shame look any Christian man in the face, seeing you have forsaken the truth, denied our Saviour Christ and His Word, and done contrary to your own oath and writing? With what countenance will you appear before the judgment-seat of Christ, and answer to your oath made first to King Henry VIII, and afterward unto King Edward VI, his son?' "

The interview, which began in this extraordinary manner, terminated as might have been expected. After several sharp arguments and wrangles, in which the Suffolk Rector showed himself more than a match for the Bishop of Winchester, Taylor was committed to the King's Bench prison. On hearing his committal, he kneeled down, and holding up both his hands, said "Good Lord, I thank Thee. From the tyranny of the Bishop of Rome, and all his detestable errors, idolatries, and abominations, good Lord, deliver us. And God be praised for good King Edward."

Rowland Taylor lay in prison almost two years, and spent most of his time in prayer, reading the Scriptures, and writing. He had also opportunities of exhorting and addressing the prisoners. How much he saw of the other Reformers who were in prison at the same time, is not quite clear. It is certain, however, that he was very often in company of the famous John Bradford, and told his friends that God had sent him to a prison, where he "found an angel of God to comfort him." It is also highly probable that he had occasional interviews with the illustrious Reformers, Hooper, Rogers, Ferrar, and Saunders, who all, like himself, were finally burned at the stake.

The end of Rowland Taylor's weary imprisonment came at last. On the 22nd of January, 1555, he was brought before the Lord Chancellor, Bishop Gardiner, and other Commissioners, and subjected to a lengthy examination. To go into the details of all that was said on this occasion would be wearisome and unprofitable. The whole affair was conducted with the same gross unfairness and partiality which characterized all the proceedings against the English Reformers, and the result, as a matter of course, was the good man's condemnation. To use his own words, in a letter to a friend, he was pronounced a heretic because he defended the marriage of priests, and denied the doctrine of transubstantiation. Never let it be forgotten in these days, that the denial of any corporal presence of Christ's Body and Blood in the elements of bread and wine at the Lord's Supper, was the turning-point which decided the fate of our martyred Reformers. If they gave way on that point they might have lived. Because they would not admit any corporal presence they died. These things are recorded for our learning.

On the 30th of January, 1555, Taylor, together with Bradford, Ferrar and Saunders, was called to appear before the Bishops of Winchester, Norwich, London, Salisbury, and Durham. They were all four charged with heresy, and schism, and required to answer determinately whether they would submit themselves to the Bishop of Rome, and abjure their errors. On their refusal they were condemned to death. "For this," says Foxe, "they gave God thanks, and stoutly said unto the Bishops, 'We doubt not but God, the righteous Judge, will require our blood at your hands, and the proudest of you all shall repent this receiving again of Antichrist, and your tyranny that ye now show against the flock of Christ.' " On the evening of this day, Taylor was sent to the Compter prison, and parted from his brethren.

On the 4th of February, Bonner, Bishop of London, came to the Compter prison, and formally degraded Taylor from the office of priest, with many absurd ceremonies, of which Foxe supplies a ludicrous description. The night after his degradation, his wife and his son Thomas were permitted to visit and sup with him, and after supper they parted, with much affection and many tears. The next day, the fifth of February, he set out on his journey to Hadleigh, in order that he might be burned in the presence of his parishioners. The circumstances of his departure from London are so touchingly described by Foxe, that I think it best to let the old historian speak for himself.

"On the next morrow after that Dr Taylor had supped with his wife in the Compter prison, which was the 5th day of February, the Sheriff of London, with his officers came to the Compter by two o'clock in the morning, and so brought forth Dr Taylor; and without any light led him to the Woolsack, an inn without Aldgate. Dr Taylor's wife, suspecting that her husband should that night be carried away, watched all night in St Botolph's Church porch, beside Aldgate, having with her two children, the one named Elizabeth, of thirteen years of age, whom, being left without father or mother, Dr Taylor had brought up of alms from three years old; the other named Mary, Dr Taylor's own daughter.

'Now when the Sheriff and his company came against St Botolph's Church, Elizabeth cried, saying, 'O my dear father! Mother, mother: here is my father led away!' Then cried his wife, 'Rowland, Rowland: where art thou?' for it was a very dark morning, that the one could not see the other. Dr Taylor answered, 'Dear wife, I am here,' and stayed. The Sheriff's men would have led him forth, but the Sheriff said, 'Stay a little, masters, I pray you, and let him speak to his wife;' and so they stayed.

"Then came she to him, and he took his daughter Mary in his arms, and he, his wife, and Elizabeth kneeled down and said the Lord's Prayer. At which sight the Sheriff wept apace, and so did divers others of the company. After they had prayed, he rose up and kissed his wife, and shook her by the hand, and said, 'Farewell, my dear wife: be of good comfort, for I am quiet in my conscience. God shall raise up a father for my children.' And then he kissed his daughter Mary, and said, 'God bless thee, and make thee His servant;' and, kissing Elizabeth, he said, 'God bless thee.

I pray you all stand strong and steadfast to Christ and His Word, and keep you from idolatry.' Then said his wife, 'God be with thee, dear Rowland: I will, with God's grace, meet thee at Hadleigh.'

"And so was he led forth to the Woolsack, and his wife followed him. As soon as they came to the Woolsack, he was put into a chamber, wherein he was kept, with four yeoman of the guard and the Sheriff's men. Dr Taylor, as soon as he was come into the chamber, fell down on his knees, and gave himself wholly to prayer. The Sheriff then, seeing Dr Taylor's wife there, would in no case grant her to speak any more with her husband; but gently desired her to go to his house, and take it as her own, and promised her she should lack nothing, and sent two officers to conduct her thither. Notwithstanding, she desired to go to her mother's, whither the officers led her, and charged her mother to keep her there till they came again."

Rowland Taylor's journey from London to Hadleigh is minutely described by Foxe. He travelled on horseback, according to the custom of those days, and stopped at Brentwood, Chelmsford, and Lavenham. "All the way he was joyful and merry, as one that accounted himself going to a most pleasant banquet or bridal." But we must content ourselves with the account of the closing scene in the worthy martyr's history, which shall be given in Foxe's own words:

On the 9th February, 1555 (the same day that Bishop Hooper was burnt at Gloucester), "the Sheriff and his company led Dr Taylor towards Hadleigh; and coming within two miles of Hadleigh, he desired for somewhat to light off his horse; which done, he leaped, and fet a frisk, or twain, as men commonly do in dancing. 'Why, master Doctor,' quoth the Sheriff, 'how do you now?' He answered, 'Well, God be praised, good master Sheriff, never better; for now I know I am almost at home. I lack not past two stiles to go over, and I am at even at my Father's house. But, master Sheriff,' said he, 'shall we not go through Hadleigh?' 'Yes,' said the Sheriff, 'you shall go through Hadleigh.' Then said he, 'O good Lord, I thank Thee! I shall yet once ere I die, see my flock whom Thou, Lord, knowest I have most heartily loved and truly taught. Good Lord, bless them, and keep them steadfast in Thy Word and truth.'

"When they were now come to Hadleigh, and came riding over the bridge, at the bridge foot waited a poor man with five small children, who, when he saw Dr Taylor, he and his children fell down upon their knees and held up their hands, and cried with a loud voice, and said, 'O dear father and good shepherd, Dr Taylor, God help and succour thee, as thou hast many a time succoured me and my poor children.' Such witness had this servant of God of his virtuous and charitable alms-giving in his lifetime; for God would now the poor should testify of his good deeds to his singular comfort, to the example of others, and confusion of his persecutors and tyrannous adversaries. For the Sheriff and others that led him to death were wonderfully astonished at this, and the Sheriff sore rebuked the poor man for so crying. The streets of Hadleigh were beset on both sides the way with men and women of the town and country who waited to see him; whom, when they beheld so led to death, with weeping eyes and lamentable voices they cried, saying one to another, 'Ah, good Lord, there goeth our good shepherd from us, that so faithfully hath taught us, so fatherly hath cared for us, and so godly hath governed us. O merciful God! What shall we poor scattered lambs do? What shall come of this most wicked world? Good Lord, strengthen him and comfort him,' with such other most lamentable and piteous voices. Wherefore the people were sore rebuked by the Sheriff and the catchpoles, his men, that led him. And Dr Taylor evermore said to the people, I have preached to you God's Word and truth, and am come this day to seal it with my blood.'

"Coming against the almshouses, which he well knew, he cast to the poor people money which remained of that which good people had given him in time of his imprisonment. As for his living, they took it from him at his first going to prison, so that he was sustained all the time of his imprisonment by the charitable alms of good people that visited him. Therefore the money that now remained he put in a glove ready for the same purpose, and, as is said, gave it to the poor almsmen standing at their doors to see him. And coming to the last of the almshouses, and not seeing the poor that there dwelt ready at their doors as the others were, he asked, 'Is the blind man and blind woman that dwelt here alive?' It was answered, 'Yea, they are within.' Then threw he glove and all in at the window, and so rode forth.

"At the last, coming to Aldham Common, the place assigned where he should suffer, and seeing a great multitude of people gathered thither, he asked, 'What place is this, and what meaneth it that so much people are gathered hither?' It was answered, 'It is Aldham Common, the place where you must suffer, and the people are come to look upon you.' Then he said, 'Thanked be God, I am even at home;' and so alighted from his horse, and rent the hood from his head.

"Now was his hair cut short and ill-favouredly, and clipped much as a man would clip a fool's head; which cost the *good* Bishop Bonner had bestowed upon him when he degraded him. But when the people saw his reverend and ancient face, with a long white beard, they burst out with weeping tears, and cried, saying, 'God save thee, good Dr Taylor! Jesus Christ strengthen thee; the Holy Ghost comfort thee,' with such other like godly wishes. Then would he have spoken to the people, but the yeoman of the guard were so busy about him, that as soon as he opened his mouth, one or other thrust a tipstaff into his mouth, and would in no wise permit him to speak.

"Dr Taylor, perceiving that he could not be permitted to speak, sat down, and seeing one named Soyce, he called him, and said, 'Soyce, I pray thee come and pull off my boots, and take them for thy labour. Thou hast long looked for them, now take them.' Then rose he up, and put off his clothes unto his shirt, and gave them away; which done, he said with a loud voice, 'Good people, I have taught you nothing but God's Holy Word, and those lessons that I have taken out of God's blessed Book, the Holy Bible; and I am come hither this day to seal it with my blood.' With that word, a certain yeoman of the guard, who had used Dr Taylor very cruelly all the way, gave him a great stroke upon the head with a waster[1], and said, 'Is that the keeping of thy promise, thou heretic? Then he, seeing they would not permit him to speak, kneeled down and prayed, and a poor woman that was among the people stepped in and prayed with him, but they thrust her away, and threatened to tread her down with horses; notwithstanding, she would not remove, but abode and prayed with him. When he had prayed, he

[1] a cudgel.

went to the stake and kissed it, and set himself into a pitch-barrel, which they had set for him to stand in, and so stood with his back upright against the stake, with his hands folded together, and his eyes toward heaven, and so he continually prayed."

After some painful delay, and some miserable insults from the Popish helpers who were assisting, the fire was lighted. Then says Foxe, "Dr Taylor, holding up both his hands, called upon God, and said, 'Merciful Father of heaven, for Jesus Christ my Saviour's sake, receive my soul into Thy hands.' So stood he still, without either crying or moving, until one struck him on the head with a halbert, so that his brains fell out, and the dead corpse fell down into the fire.

Thus died one of the best and bravest of the English martyrs. An old rude stone still marks the spot where he was burned, in the midst of an enclosed field, which once formed part of Aldham Common. It bears the following quaint but pithy inscription:

"1555.

"Dr Taylor, in defending that
which was good, at this
place left his blood."

In the year 1819 another and more pretentious monument was erected on the same spot, with a long poetical inscription written by the Rector of Hadleigh. But the martyr's history is still remembered in the parish, without the aid of stones and monuments. "Being dead, he yet speaketh."

Taylor's last parting wishes to his wife and family and parishioners were written in a book which he gave his son as a parting legacy, only five days before his martyrdom. They can hardly fail to interest the reader.

"I say to my wife and to my children, The Lord gave you unto me, and the Lord hath taken me from you and you from me: blessed be the name of the Lord! I believe that they are blessed which die in the Lord. God careth for sparrows, and for the hairs of our heads. I have ever found Him more faithful and favourable than is any father or husband. Trust ye, therefore, in Him by the means of our dear Saviour Christ's merits. Believe, love, fear, and obey Him: pray to Him, for He hath promised to help. Count me not dead, for I shall certainly live and never die. I go before, and you shall follow after, to our long home. I go to the rest of my children, Susan, George, Ellen, Robert, and Zachary. I have bequeathed you to the only Omnipotent.

"I say to my dear friends of Hadleigh, and to all others which have heard me preach, that I depart hence with a quiet conscience as touching my doctrine, for the which I pray you thank God with me. For I have, after my little talent, declared to others those lessons that I gathered out of God's Book, the blessed Bible. 'Therefore, if I, or an angel from heaven, should preach to you any other Gospel than that ye have received,' God's great curse be upon that preacher!

"Beware, for God's sake, that ye deny not God, neither decline from the word of faith, lest God decline from you, and so do ye everlastingly perish. For God's sake beware of Popery, for though it appear to have in it unity, yet the same is vanity and anti-Christianity, and not in Christ's faith and verity.

"Beware of the sin against the Holy Ghost, now after such a light opened so plainly and simply, truly, thoroughly and generally to all England.

"The Lord grant all men His good and Holy Spirit, increase of His wisdom, contemning the wicked world, hearty desire to be with God and the heavenly company; though Jesus Christ, our only Mediator, Advocate, Righteousness, Life, Sanctification, and Hope. Amen. Amen. Pray. Pray.

"Rowland Taylor, departing hence in sure hope, without all doubting of eternal salvation. I thank God, my heavenly Father, through Jesus Christ, my certain Saviour. Amen. 5th of February, anno 1555.

" 'The Lord is my Light and my Salvation, whom then shall I fear? God is He that justifieth: who is he that can condemn?

In Thee, O Lord, have I trusted: let me never be confounded.' "

Does any one wish to know whether the Church of Rome is infallible? Let him carefully study the history of such martyrdoms as that of Rowland Taylor. Of all the stupid and suicidal mistakes that the Romish Church ever made, none was greater than the mistake of burning the Reformers. It cemented the work of the Reformation, and made Englishmen Protestants by thousands. When plain Englishmen saw the Church of Rome so cruelly wicked and Protestants so brave, they ceased to doubt on which side was the truth. May the memory of our martyred Reformers never be forgotten in England until the Lord comes!

HUGH LATIMER: BISHOP AND MARTYR

The name of Bishop Latimer is well known to all readers of English Church history. There are, probably, few who have not read that more than three hundred years ago there was such a Queen of England as "Bloody Mary," and that men were burnt alive in her reign because they would not give up Protestantism, and that one of these men was Bishop Latimer.

But English Churchmen ought to know these things better in the present day. They ought to become thoroughly familiar with the lives, the acts, and the opinions of the leading English Reformers. Their *names* ought to be something better than hackneyed ornaments to point a platform speech. Their *principles* ought no longer to be vague, hazy shadows "looming in the distance," but something clear, distinct, and well-defined before our mind's eyes. My desire is, that men may understand that the best interests of this country are bound up with Protestantism. My wish is, that men may write on their hearts that the well-being of England depends not on commerce, or clever politicians, or steam, or armies, or navies, or gold, or iron, or coal, or corn, but on the maintenance of the principles of the English Reformation.

The times we live in call loudly for the diffusion of knowledge about English Church history. Opinions are boldly broached nowadays of so startling a nature, that they make a man rub his eyes, and say, "Where am I?" A state of feeling is growing up among us about Romanism and Protestantism, which, to say the least, is most unhealthy. It has increased, is increasing, and ought to be diminished. Nothing is so likely to check this state of feeling as the production of a few plain facts. If you want to convince a Scotsman, they say you must give him a long argument. If you want to convince an Englishman, you must give him plain facts. Facts are the principal commodity I have brought together in this biographical paper. If anyone expects to find in these pages private speculation, or oratorical display, I am afraid he will be disappointed; but if any one likes plain facts, I think I shall be able to supply him with a few.

Does any reader doubt who is a true member of the Church of England? Are you perplexed by the rise and progress of what are foolishly called 'Church views'? Come with me to-day, and pay a visit to one of the Fathers of the English Church. Let us put into the witness box one of the most honest and out-spoken bishops of the days of the English Reformation. Let us examine the life and opinions of good old Latimer.

Does any reader doubt what is the true character of the Church of Rome? Are you bewildered by some of those plausible gentlemen who tell you there is no fundamental difference between the Anglican and Romish Churches? Are you puzzled by that intense yearning after so-called 'Catholic' principles, which distinguishes some misguided Churchmen, and which exhibits itself in 'Catholic' teaching, 'Catholic' ceremonies, 'Catholic' books of devotion, and 'Catholic' architecture? Come with me to-day, and turn over a few old pages in English history. Let us see what England actually was when Romish teachers instructed the English people, and had things all their own way. Let us see what the Church of Rome does when she has complete power. Let us see how she treats the friends of an open Bible, of private judgment, and of justification by faith. Let us see how the Church of Rome dealt with Bishop Latimer.

I. In examining the history of Bishop Latimer, *the times in which he lived* demand attentive consideration. It is impossible to form a just estimate of a man's conduct unless we know the circumstances in which he is placed, and the difficulties with which he has to contend. No one is aware of the whole extent of our obligations to the noble band of English Reformers, who is not acquainted with the actual state of England when they began their work, and the amazing disadvantages under which that work was carried on.

Latimer was born in the reign of Henry VII. He lived through the reigns of Henry VIII and Edward VI, and was put to death in the reign of Queen Mary. He began life at a period when Popery bore undisputed sway in this country. He witnessed the beginning of the breach between Henry VIII and Rome, and the establishment of a transition state of religion in England. He lived to see the full development of Protestantism under Edward VI, and the compilation of a Liturgy and Articles very slightly differing from those we have at this day. About each of these three periods I must say a few words.

(a) The first period of Latimer's life, when Popery was supreme in England, was a period of *utter spiritual darkness*. The depth of superstition in which our worthy forefathers were sunk is enough to make one's hair stand on end. No doubt there were many Lollards, and followers of Wycliffe, scattered over the land, who held the truth, and were the salt of the nation. But the fierce persecution with which these good men were generally assailed prevented their making much progress. They barely maintained their own ground. And as for the mass of the population, gross darkness covered their minds.

Most of the priests and teachers of religion were themselves profoundly ignorant of everything they ought to have known. They were generally ordained without any adequate examination as to learning or character. Many of them, though they could read their breviaries, knew nothing whatever of the Bible. Some, according to Strype the historian, were scarcely able to say the Lord's Prayer, and not a few were unable to repeat the Ten Commandments. The prayers of the Church were in the Latin language, which hardly anybody understood. Preaching there was scarcely any, and what there was, was grossly unscriptural and unedifying.

Huge nests of ordained men were dotted over the face of England, in the shape of Abbeys and Monasteries. The inhabitants of these beautiful buildings were seldom very holy and self-denying, and were often men of most profligate and disreputable lives. Their morals were just what might have been expected from "fulness of bread and abundance of idleness." They did next to nothing for the advancement of learning. They did nothing for the spread of true religion. Two things only they cared for, and those two were to fill their own pockets, and to keep up their own power. For the one purpose they persuaded weak and dying people to give money and lands to the Church under the specious pretence that they would in this way be delivered from purgatory, and their faith proved by their good works. For the other purpose they claimed to hold the keys of the kingdom of heaven. To *them* confession of sins must be made. Without *their* absolution and extreme unction, no man could be saved. Without *their* Masses no soul could be redeemed from purgatory. In short, *they* were practically the mediators between Christ and man; and to injure them was the highest offence and sin. Old Fuller tells us for example, that in 1489 a certain Italian got an immense sum of money in England, by "having power from the Pope to absolve people from usury, simony, theft, manslaughter, fornication, and adultery, and all crimes whatsoever, except smiting the clergy and conspiring against the Pope." (i. 532. Tegg's edition.) Such were Romish priests in Latimer's youth, when Popery was last rampant in England. To say that they were generally ignorant, covetous, sensual, and despotic tyrants over the souls and bodies of men, is not saying one jot more than the truth.

When priests in Latimer's youth were men of this stamp, we shall not be surprised to hear that *the people* were utterly ignorant of true religion. It would have been miraculous indeed if it had been otherwise, when they had neither sound preaching to hear, nor Bibles to read. A New Testament could not be bought for less than £2 16s. 3d., and the buyer was in danger of being considered a heretic for purchasing it. The Christianity of the vast majority was naturally enough a mere name and form. The Sabbath was a day of sport and pastime, and not a day of solemn worship. Not one in a hundred perhaps could have rightly answered the question, 'What shall I do to be saved? or given the slightest account of justification, regeneration, sanctification, the office of Christ, or the work of the Spirit. A man's only idea of the way to heaven generally was, to do as the priest told him, and to belong to "the true Church!" Thus the blind led the blind, and all wallowed in the ditch together.

All the practical religion that the mass of the laity possessed, consisted in prayers to the Virgin Mary and saints, paying the priests to say Masses, pilgrimages to holy places, and adoration of images and relics. The list of their superstitious practices would make an appalling catalogue. They hastened to the church for holy water before a thunderstorm. They resorted to St Rooke in times of pestilence. They prayed to St Pernel in an ague. Young women, desiring to be married, sought the help of St Nicholas. Wives, weary of their husbands, betook themselves to St Uncumber. One hundred thousand pilgrims visited the tomb of St Thomas à Becket, at Canterbury, in one year in order to help their souls towards heaven. In one year at Canterbury Cathedral, there was offered at Christ's altar £3 2s. 6d.; on the Virgin Mary's, £63 5s. 6d.; and on Thomas à Becket's, £832 12s. 3d. The *images* worshipped were often gross cheats as well as idols. The *relics* worshipped were as monstrous and absurd as the images. As to the bones of saints, there were whole heaps which had been venerated for years, which proved at length to be bones of deer and pigs. These are dreadful things to tell, but they ought to be known. All these things the Church of Rome knew, connived at, sanctioned, defended, taught, and enforced on her members. This was the state of religion in England in the early years of the 16th century, when the English Reformers were raised up. This was English Christianity in the childhood and youth of Hugh Latimer!

(*b*) The second period of Latimer's life, during which England was in a state of transition between Romanism and Protestantism, presents many curious features.

We see, on the one hand, a reformation of religion begun by a King from motives which, to say the least, were not spiritual. It would be absurd to suppose that a sensual tyrant like Henry VIII came to a breach with the Pope for any other reason than that the Pope crossed his will. We see his pretended scruples about his marriage with Catherine of Aragon bringing him into communication with Cranmer and Latimer. We see him, *at one time*, so far guided by the advice of these good men, that, like Herod, he does many things that are right, and likely to advance the cause of the Gospel. He makes Cranmer Archbishop of Canterbury, and shows him favour to the end of his days. He allows the Bible to be printed in England and placed in churches. He commands images to be broken, and puts down many gross superstitions. He boldly denies the doctrine of the Pope's supremacy. He dissolves the monasteries, and puts to open shame the wickedness of their inmates. All this we see and are thankful. We see him, *at another time*, defending Popish dogmas, and burning men who, like the martyr Lambert, denied them. We see him putting forth the famous Six Articles, which re-asserted transubstantiation, private Masses, clerical celibacy, vows of chastity, auricular confession, and the denial of the cup to the laity. Worst of all, we see in him the marks of a proud, self-willed, sensual man all his life long, and an utter want of evidence that his heart was ever right in the sight of God. The employment of a man who was guilty of such inconsistencies, to do God's work, is among the deep things of God's providence. We cannot understand it. We must wait.

Turning, on the other hand, from Henry VIII to the first English Reformers, we see in them strong indications of what Fuller calls "a twilight religion." We see them putting forth books in Henry VIII's reign, which, though an immense improvement and advance upon Romish teaching, still contain some things which are not Scriptural. Such were "The Necessary Erudition," and the "Institution of a Christian Man." We see them, however, gradually growing in spiritual knowledge, perhaps unawares to themselves, and specially as to the error of transubstantiation. We see them continually checked and kept back, partly by the arbitrary conduct of the King, partly by the immense difficulty of working side by side with a Popish party in the Church, and partly by the great ignorance of the parochial clergy. Nevertheless, on comparing the end of Henry VIII's reign with the beginning, we see plain proof that much ground was gained. We learn to admire the overruling power of God, who can use a Henry VIII just as He did a Nebuchadnezzar or Sennacherib, for the accomplishment of His own purposes. And last, but not least, we learn to admire the patient perseverance of the Reformers. Though they had but little strength, they used it. Though they had but a small door open, they entered in by it. Though they had but one talent, they laid it out heartily for God, and did not bury it in the ground. Though they had but a little light, they lived fully up to it. If they could not do what they would, they did what they could, and were blessed in their deed. Such was the second period of Latimer's life. Never let it be forgotten that, at this time, the foundations of the Church of England were excavated, and vast heaps of rubbish removed out of the way of the builders who were to follow. Viewed in this light, it will always be an interesting period to the student of Church history.

(c) The last period of Latimer's life, which comprises the reign of Edward VI, is in many respects very different from the two periods to which I have already adverted. The cause of English Protestantism made immense progress during Edward's short but remarkable tenure of power. It was truly said of him by Hooker, that "He died young, but lived long, if life be action." Released from the bondage of a tyrannical King's interference, Cranmer and his friends went forward in the work of religious reformation with rapid strides. Bonner and Gardiner were no longer allowed to keep them back. Refusing to take part in the good work, these two Popish prelates were deposed and put to silence. Faithful men, like Ridley and Hooper, were placed on the episcopal bench. An immense clearance of Popish ceremonies was effected. A Liturgy was compiled, which differed very slightly from our present Prayer-book. The forty-two Articles of religion were drawn up, which form the basis of our own thirty-nine. The first book of Homilies was put forth, in order to supply the want of preachers. An accuracy and clearness of doctrinal statement was arrived at, which had hitherto been unknown. Learned foreigners, like Martin Bucer and Peter Martyr, were invited to visit England and appointed Regius Professors of Divinity at Oxford and Cambridge. How much further the Reformers might have carried the work of reformation, if they had had time, it is useless now to conjecture. Judging by the changes they effected in a very few years, they would probably have made our Church as nearly perfect as a visible Church can be, if they had not been stopped by Edward's premature death.

There was, however, one thing which the Reformers of Edward VI's reign could not accomplish. They could not change the hearts of the parochial clergy. Thousands of clergymen continued to hold office in the Church of England, who had no sympathy with the proceedings of Cranmer and his party. There was no getting rid of these worthies, for they were ready to promise anything, sign anything, and swear anything, in order to keep their livings. But while they yielded compliance to Cranmer's injunctions and commands, they were graceless, ignorant, and semi-Papists at heart. The questions which Bishop Hooper found it necessary to put to the dean, prebendaries, and clergy of the diocese of Gloucester on his first visitation, and the answers which he received, furnish us, as we have seen, with a sad illustration of the state of English clergymen in Edward VI's time.

Facts such as these are painful and astounding; but it is most important that we should know them. They explain at once the ease with which Bloody Mary restored Popery when she came to the throne. Parochial clergymen like those just described were not likely to offer any resistance to her wishes. Facts such as these throw great light on the position of Cranmer and the reformers of Edward VI's days. We probably have little idea of the immense difficulties both within and without which beset them. Above all, facts such as these give us some idea of the condition of religion in England even in the brightest portion of Latimer's times. If things like these were to be seen when Latimer was an old man, what must have been seen when he was young! If ignorance like this prevailed under Edward VI, how thick must the darkness have been under Henry VIII!

I must dwell no longer on the subject of Latimer's times. The subject has been already exhausted in Hooper's biography, and I do not wish to weary my readers by a dry and tedious repetition of facts. But I firmly believe that a knowledge of these facts is absolutely essential to a right understanding of the English Reformation, and I therefore hope that the few which I have given will not prove useless.

On calm consideration, I trust my readers will agree with me, that it is the height of absurdity to say, as some do nowadays, that this country has been a loser by getting rid of Popery. It is really astonishing to hear the nonsense talked about "merry England in the olden times," the "mediæval piety," the "ages of faith," and the "devout habits of our Catholic forefathers."

Walter Scott's fascinating writings and Pugin's beautiful architectural designs, have lent a false glare to Romanism in England, and induced many to doubt whether our Reformation really was a gain. The state of English society, which Scott has sometimes made so interesting by his pen, and Pugin by his pencil, is a far more beautiful thing in poems and pictures than it ever was in honest reality. Depend upon it, "Distance lends enchantment to the view." We may rest satisfied that Netley, and Glastonbury, and Bury, and Fountains, and Melrose, and Bolton Abbeys, are much more useful now in ruins than they ever were in Henry

VII's days. Few Englishmen probably have the least idea how much we have gained by the Reformation. We have gained light, knowledge, morality, and religious liberty. Few have any clear idea of the fruits which grew on the tree of Popery when last it flourished in England. Those fruits were ignorance, superstition, immorality, and priestly tyranny. God was angered, souls were lost, and the devil was pleased.

I trust again my readers will feel with me, that it is most unfair to suppose that the acts and writings of the English Reformers under Henry VIII are any real criterion of their matured opinions. It is as unfair as it would be to measure the character of a grown-up man by his sayings and doings when he was a child. Cranmer and his helpers under Henry VIII were in a state of spiritual childhood. They saw many points in religion through a glass darkly. It was not till the reign of Edward VI that they put away childish things. We must beware, therefore, lest any man deceive us by artfully-chosen quotations drawn from works published in the beginning of the English Reformation. Judge the Reformers, if you will, by their writings in the reign of Edward VI, but not by their writings in the reign of Henry VIII.

I trust, lastly, my readers will agree with me, that it is most unreasonable to decry the early English Reformers, as men who did not go far enough. Such charges are easily made, but those who make them seldom consider the enormous obstacles the Reformers had to surmount, and the enormous evils they had to remove. It is nonsense to suppose they had nothing more to do than to pare the moss off an old building, and whitewash it afresh. They had to take down an old decayed house, and rebuild it from the very ground. It is nonsense to criticize their proceedings, as if they voyaged over a smooth sea, with a fair wind, and a clear course. On the contrary, they had to pilot the ship of true religion through a narrow and difficult strait, against current, wind and tide. Put all their difficulties together, the arbitrary, profligate character of Henry VIII, and the tender years of Edward VI, the general ignorance of the population—the bitter enmity of dispossessed monks and friars—the open opposition of many of the Bishops, and the secret indifference of a vast proportion of the clergy, put all these things together, and weigh them well; and then I think you will not lightly regard the work that the early

Reformers did. For my own part, so far from wondering that they did so little, I wonder rather that they did so much. I marvel at their firmness. I am surprised at their success. I see immense results produced by comparatively weak instruments, and I can only account for it by saying, that "God was with them of a truth."

II. The next branch of my subject to which I shall invite the attention of my readers is *the story of Bishop Latimer's life*.

Hugh Latimer was born about the year 1485, at Thurcaston, near Mount Sorrel, in the county of Leicester. He has left such a graphic account of his father and family, in one of his sermons preached before Edward VI, that I must in justice give it in his own words. He says "My father was a yeoman, and had no lands of his own. He had only a farm of three or four pounds a year at the uttermost, and hereupon he tilled so much as kept half a dozen men. He had walk for a hundred sheep, and my mother milked thirty kine. He was able, and did find the King a harness, with himself and his horse, while he came to the place where he should receive the King's wages. I can remember that I buckled his harness, when he went to Blackheath Field.[1] He kept me to school, or else I had not been able to have preached before the King's majesty now. He married my sisters with five pounds apiece, and brought them up in godliness and the fear of God. He kept hospitality for his poor neighbours, and some alms he gave to the poor." (Works, i. 101. Parker Society's edition.) Such is the good Bishop's homely account of his own family. It is only fair to observe that Latimer is one among the thousand examples on record, that England, with all its faults, is a country where a man may begin very low, and yet live to rise very high.

Latimer was sent to Cambridge at the age of twenty-one, and in 1510 was elected a Fellow of Clare Hall. We know very little of his early history, except the remarkable fact, which he himself has told us, that up to the age of thirty he was a most violent and bigoted Papist. Just as St Paul was not ashamed to tell men that at one time he was a "blasphemer, and a persecutor, and injurious," so the old Protestant Bishop used often to tell how he too had once been the slave of Rome. He says in one of his sermons, "I was as obstinate a Papist as any was in England,

[1] An army of Cornish rebels defeated at Blackheath in 1497.

insomuch that when I should be made bachelor of divinity, my whole oration went against Philip Melanchthon and against his opinions." (Works, i. 334.) He says in another sermon, "All the Papists think themselves to be saved by the law, and I myself was of that dangerous, perilous, and damnable opinion till I was thirty years of age. So long had I walked in darkness and the shadow of death." (ii. 137.) He says in a letter to Sir Edward Baynton, "I have thought in times past that if I had been a friar and in a cowl, I could not have been damned nor afraid of death; and by occasion of the same I have been minded many times to have been a friar, namely, when I was sore sick and diseased. Now I abhor my superstitious foolishness." (ii. 332.)

Latimer's testimony about himself is confirmed by others. It is recorded that he used to think so ill of the Reformers, that he declared the last times, the day of judgment, and the end of the world must be approaching. "Impiety," he said, "was gaining ground apace, and what lengths might not men be expected to run, when they began to question even the infallibility of the Pope?" Becon mentions that when Stafford, the divinity lecturer, delivered lectures in Cambridge, on the Bible, Latimer was sure to be present, in order to frighten and drive away the scholars. In fact his zeal for Popery was so notorious, that he was elected to the office of cross-bearer in the religious processions of the University, and discharged the duty with becoming solemnity for seven years. Such was the clay of which God formed a precious vessel meet for His work! Such were the first beginnings of one of the best and most useful of the English Reformers!

The instrument which God used in order to bring this furious Papist to a knowledge of Christ's truth, was a student named Bilney. Bilney was a contemporary of Latimer's at Cambridge, who had for some time embraced the doctrines of the Reformation, and was finally burned as a martyr at Norwich. He perceived that Latimer was a sincere and honest man, and kindly thought it possible that his zeal for Popery might arise from lack of knowledge. He, therefore, went boldly to him after his public onslaught on Melanchthon, and humbly asked to be allowed to make a private confession of his own faith. The success of this courageous step was complete. Old Latimer tells us, "I learned more by his confession than before in many years. From that time forward I began to smell the Word of God, and forsook the school doctors and such fooleries." (i. 334.) Bilney's conduct on this occasion seems to have been most praiseworthy. It ought to encourage every one to try to do good to his neighbour. It is a shining proof of the truth of the proverb, "A word spoken in season, how good is it!"

Hugh Latimer was not a man to do anything by halves. As soon as he ceased to be a zealous Papist, he began at once to be a zealous Protestant, and gave himself up, body, soul, and mind, to the work of doing good. He visited, in Bilney's company, the sick and prisoners. He commenced preaching in the University pulpits, in a style hitherto unknown in Cambridge, and soon became famous as one of the most striking and powerful preachers of the day. He stirred up hundreds of his hearers to search the Scriptures and inquire after the way of salvation. Becon, after-wards chaplain to Cranmer, and Bradford, afterwards chaplain to Ridley, both traced their conversion to his sermons. Becon has left us a remarkable description of the effects of his preaching. He says, "None, except the stiff-necked and uncircumcised in heart, went away from it without being affected with high detestation of sin, and moved unto all godliness and virtue." (Becon's Works, vol. ii. 224. Parker Society's edition.)

The consequences of this faithful discharge of ministerial duty were just what all experience might lead us to expect. There arose against Latimer a storm of persecution. Swarms of friars and doctors who had admired him when he carried the cross as a Papist, rose up against him in a body when he preached the cross like St Paul. The Bishop of Ely forbade his preaching any more in the University pulpits at Cambridge; and had he not obtained permission from Dr Barnes to preach in the church of the Augustine Friars, which was exempt from episcopal jurisdiction, he might have been silenced altogether. But the malice of his enemies did not stop here. Complaints were laid against him before Cardinal Wolsey, and he had more than once to appear before him and Tonstall, Bishop of London, on charges of heresy. Indeed, when the circumstances of the times are considered, it is wonderful that Latimer did not at this period of his life share Bilney's fate, and suffer death at the stake.

But the Lord, in whose hand our times are, had more work for

Latimer to do, and raised up for him unexpected friends in high quarters. His decided opinions in favour of Henry VIII's divorce from Catherine of Aragon brought him into communication with Dr Butts, the King's physician, and ultimately secured to him the favour and patronage of the King himself. In the year 1530 he was made one of the royal chaplains, and preached before the King several times. In the year 1531 the royal favour procured for him an appointment to the living of West Kington, near Chippenham, in Wiltshire; and, in spite of his friend Dr Butts' remonstrances, he at once left court, and went to reside upon his cure.

At West Kington Latimer was just the same man that he had been latterly at Cambridge, and found the devil just as busy an adversary in Wiltshire as he had found him in the University. In pastoral labours he was abundant. In preaching he was instant in season and out of season, both within his parish and without. This he had full authority to do, by virtue of a general licence from the University of Cambridge. But the more he did, the more angry the idle Popish clergy round West Kington became, and the more they laboured to stop his proceedings. So true is it that human nature is the same in all ages. There is generally a dog-in-the-manger spirit about a graceless minister. He neither does good himself nor likes any one else to do it for him. This was the case with the Pharisees: they "took away the key of knowledge: they entered not in themselves, and them that were entering in they hindered." (Luke xi. 52.) And as it was in the days of the Pharisees, so it was in the days of Latimer.

On one occasion the Mayor and Magistrates of Bristol, who were very friendly to him, had appointed him to preach before them on Easter Day. Public notice had been given, and everybody was looking forward to the sermon with pleasure, for Latimer was very popular in Bristol. Suddenly there came out an order from the Bishop forbidding any one to preach in Bristol without his licence. The clergy of the place waited on Latimer, and informed him of the Bishop's order, and then, knowing well that he had no such licence, told him, "that they were extremely sorry they were deprived of the pleasure of hearing an excellent discourse from him." Their hypocritical compliments and regrets were unfortunately ill-timed. Latimer had heard the whole history of the affair.

And he knew well that these smooth-tongued gentlemen were the very persons who had written to the Bishop in order to prevent his preaching.

For four years, while vicar of West Kington, the good man was subjected to a constant succession of petty worrying attacks, and attempts to stop him from doing good. He was cited to London, and brought before Archbishop Warham, and detained many months from home. He was convened before Convocation, and excommunicated and imprisoned for a time. But the protecting care of God seems to have been always round him. His enemies appear to have been marvellously restrained from carrying their malice to extremities. At length, in 1535, the King put a sudden stop to their persecution by making him Bishop of Worcester. That such a man should make such an appointment is certainly very wonderful. Some have attributed it to the influence of Lord Cromwell; some to that of the Queen Anne Boleyn; some to that of Dr Butts; some to that of Cranmer, who was always Latimer's fast friend. Such speculations are, to say the best, useless. "The King's heart is in the hand of the Lord, as the rivers of water: He turneth it whithersoever He will." (Prov. xxi. 1.) When God intends to give a good man a high office, He can always raise up a Darius to convey it to him.

The history of Latimer's episcopate is short and simple, for it only lasted four years. He was the same man in a bishop's palace that he had been in a country parsonage, or a Cambridge pulpit. Promotion did not spoil him. The mitre did not prove an extinguisher to his zeal for the Gospel. He was always faithful—always simple-minded—always about his Father's business—always labouring to do good to souls. Foxe, the historian, speaks highly of "his pains, study, readiness, and continual carefulness in teaching, preaching, exhorting, visiting, correcting, and reforming, either as his ability could serve, or the times would bear." But he adds, "the days then were so dangerous and variable that he could not in all things do what he would. Yet what he might do, that he performed to the uttermost of his strength, so that, although he could not utterly extinguish all the sparkling relics of old superstition, yet he so wrought that though they could not be taken away, yet they should be used with as little hurt and as much profit as might be."

In 1536 we find Bishop Latimer appointed by Archbishop Cranmer to preach before the Convocation of the Clergy. No doubt this appointment was made advisedly. Cranmer knew well that Latimer was just the man for the occasion. The sermons he preached are still extant, and fully justified the Archbishop's choice. Two more faithful and conscience-stirring discourses were probably never delivered to a body of ordained men. They will repay an attentive perusal. "Good brethren and fathers," he said in one place, "seeing we are here assembled, for the love of God let us do something whereby we may be known to be the children of light. Let us do somewhat, lest we, which hitherto have been judged children of the world, seem even still to be so. All men call us prelates; then seeing we be in council, let us so order ourselves that we be prelates in honour and dignity, so we may be prelates in holiness, benevolence, diligence, and sincerity."

"Lift up your heads, brethren, and look about with your eyes, and spy what things are to be reformed in the Church of England. Is it so hard, so great a matter, for you to see many abuses in the clergy, and many in the laity?" He then mentions several glaring abuses by name: the state of the Court of Arches and the Bishops' Consistories—the number of superstitious ceremonies and holidays—the worship of images and visiting of relics of saints—the lying miracles and the sale of Masses, and calls upon them to consider and amend them. He winds up all by a solemn warning of the consequence of Bishops neglecting notorious abuses. "God will come," he says, "God will come: He will not tarry long away. He will come upon such a day as we nothing look for Him, and at such an hour as we know not. He will come and cut us in pieces. He will reward us as He doth the hypocrites. He will set us where wailing shall be, my brethren—where gnashing of teeth shall be, my brethren. These be the delicate dishes prepared for the world's well-beloved children. These be the wafers and junkets provided for worldly prelates: wailing and gnashing of teeth." "Ye see, brethren, what sorrow, what punishment is provided for you if ye be worldlings. If ye will not thus be vexed, be not the children of the world. If ye will not be the children of the world, be not stricken with the love of worldly things; lean not upon them. If ye will not die eternally, live not worldly. Come, go to; leave the love of your profit: study for the glory and profit of Christ; seek in your consultations such things as pertain to Christ, and bring forth at the last somewhat that may please Christ. Feed ye tenderly, with all diligence, the flock of Christ. Preach truly the Word of God. Love the light, walk in the light, and so be ye the children of light while ye are in this world, that ye may shine in the world to come, bright as the sun, with the Father, the Son, and the Holy Ghost." (Works, vol. i. pp. 50–57.) Such was a sermon before Convocation by Latimer.

In 1537 we find Bishop Latimer placed on the Commission of Divines for the publication of a book to set forth the truth of religion; the result of which Commission was "The Institution of a Christian Man." The same year we find him putting forth some injunctions to the prior of Worcester Convent, a monastic house not yet dissolved, in which among other things, he commands the prior to have a whole Bible in English chained in the church. He orders every member of the convent to get himself an English New Testament; he directs a lecture of Scripture to be read in the convent every day, and Scripture to be read at dinner and supper. Shortly afterwards he published injunctions to the clergy of his diocese, in which he commands every one of them to provide himself with a whole Bible, or at any rate with a New Testament, and every day to read over and study one chapter, at the least. He also forbids them to set aside preaching for any manner of observance, ceremonies, or processions, and enjoins them to instruct the children in their respective parishes. All these facts are deeply instructive. They show us what an Augean stable an English diocese was in Henry VIII's day, and what enormous difficulties a reforming Bishop had to overcome.

In 1538 we find Latimer pleading with Lord Cromwell that Great Malvern Abbey might not be entirely suppressed. He suggests that it should be kept up, "not for monkery," which he says, "God forbid," but "to maintain teaching, preaching, study, and prayer;" and he asks whether it would be good policy to have two or three of the old monastic houses in every county set apart for such purposes. This was a very wise design, and shows great foresight of the country's wants. Had it been carried into effect, Durham, St Bees, St Aidan's, Lampeter, King's College, London, and the London College of Divinity, would have been unnecessary. The rapacity of Henry VIII's courtiers, who had an amazing appetite for the property of the suppressed abbeys, made the suggestion useless.

In 1539 Bishop Latimer's episcopate was brought to an end by the enactment of the Six Articles already referred to, in which some of the leading tenets of Romanism were authoritatively maintained. He strenuously withstood the passing of this Act, in opposition to the King and the Parliament; and the result was that he was compelled to resign his Bishopric. It is related, that on the day when this happened, when he came back from the House of Lords to his lodgings, he threw off his robes, and leaping up, declared to those who stood about him, that he found himself lighter than he had been for some time.

The next eight years of Latimer's life appear to have passed away in forced silence and in retirement. We read little of anything that he did. We do not exactly know where he spent his time, and whether he returned to his old living at West Kington or not. The probability is, that he was regarded as a dangerous and suspected man, and had much difficulty in preserving his life. The only certain fact we know is, that he was at length committed to prison as a heretic, and spent the last year of Henry VIII's reign in confinement in the Tower.

When Edward VI came to the throne, in 1547, Latimer was at once released from prison, and treated with every mark of respect. His old Bishopric of Worcester was offered to him, and the House of Commons presented an address to the Protector Somerset, earnestly requesting that he might be reappointed. Old age and increasing infirmities made Latimer decline the proffered dignity, and he spent the next six years of his life without any office, but certainly not as an idle man. His chief residence during these six years was with his old friend and ally, Archbishop Cranmer, under the hospitable roof of Lambeth Palace. While here, he took an active part in all the measures adopted for carrying forward the Protestant Reformation. He assisted Cranmer in composing the first book of Homilies, and was also one of the divines appointed to reform the Ecclesiastical Law, a work which was never completed. All this time he generally preached twice every Sunday. In the former part of Edward VI's reign, he preached constantly before the King. In the latter part he went to and fro in the midland counties of England, preaching wherever his services seemed to be most wanted, and especially in Lincolnshire. This was perhaps the most useful period of his life. No one of the Reformers probably sowed the seeds of sound Protestant doctrine so widely and effectually among the middle and lower classes as Latimer. The late Mr Southey bears testimony to this: he says, "Latimer, more than any other man, promoted the Reformation by his preaching."

The untimely death of Edward VI and the accession of Queen Mary to the English throne in 1553, put an end to Latimer's active exertions on behalf of the Gospel. Henceforward he was called to glorify Christ by suffering, and not by doing. The story of his sufferings, and the noble courage with which he endured them is admirably told in "Foxe's Martyrs," a book which all churchmen in these days ought to study.

As soon as Queen Mary came to the throne, one of the first acts of her Government was the apprehension of the leading English Reformers: and Latimer was among the first for whom a warrant was issued. The Queen's messenger found him doing his Master's work as a preacher in Warwickshire, but quite prepared for prison. He had received notice of what was coming six hours before the messenger arrived, from a good man named John Careless, and might easily have escaped; but he refused to avail himself of the opportunity. He said, "I go as willingly to London at this present, being called by my Prince to render a reckoning of my doctrine, as ever I went to any place in the world. And I do not doubt but that God, as He hath made me worthy to preach His Word to two excellent princes, so He will enable me to witness the same unto the third." In this spirit he rode cheerfully up to London, and said, as he passed through Smithfield, where heretics were generally burned, "Smithfield has long groaned for me."

Latimer was at once committed to the Tower, in company with Cranmer, Ridley, and Bradford, and for want of room, all the four were confined in one chamber. There these four martyrs, to use old Latimer's words, 'did together read over the New Testament with great deliberation and painful study," and unanimously agreed that transubstantiation was not to be found in it. From the Tower the three Bishops were removed to Oxford, in 1554; and there, in 1555, Latimer and Ridley were burnt alive at the stake as obstinate heretics.

The old Bishop's behaviour in prison was answerable to his previous life. For two long years he never lost his spirits, and his faith and patience never failed him. Much of his time was spent in reading the Bible. He says himself, "I read the New Testament over seven times while I was in prison." Much of his time was spent in prayer. Augustine Bernher, his faithful servant, tells us that he often continued kneeling so long that he was not able to get up from his knees without help. Three things he used especially to mention in his prayers at this time. One was, that as God had appointed him to be a preacher and professor of His Word, so He would give him grace to stand to His doctrine till his death. Another was, that God would of His mercy restore the Gospel of Christ to the realm once again; he often repeated these two words, "once again." The third was, that God would preserve the Princess Elizabeth, and make her a comfort to England. It is a striking fact, that all of these three prayers were fully granted.

Latimer's conduct at his various trials and examinations before his Popish persecutors, was in some respects wiser and better than that of the other martyrs. He knew well enough that his death was determined on, and he was quite right. Gardiner, the Popish Bishop of Winchester, had said openly, that "he would have the axe laid at the root of the tree: the Bishops and most powerful preachers ought certainly to die." Bonner, the Popish Bishop of London, had said, "God do so to Bonner, and more also, if one of the heretics escape me." Acting on this impression, Latimer told Ridley before the trial that he should say little. "They talk of a free disputation," said he, "but their argument will be as it was with their forefathers: 'We have a law, and by our law he ought to die.' " Acting on his impression, he did little at his various trials but make a simple profession of his faith. He refused to be led away into lengthy discussions about the opinions of the Fathers, like Cranmer and Ridley. He told his judges plainly, that "the Fathers might be deceived in some points,' and that he only "believed them when they said true, and had Scripture with them!" A wiser and truer remark about the Fathers was probably never made.

The death of old Latimer is so beautifully described by Foxe, that I cannot do better than give the account as nearly as possible in his words. I certainly shall not try to spoil it by any additions of my own, though I must abridge it considerably.

"The place appointed for the execution (says Foxe) was on the north side of Oxford, in the ditch over against Balliol College. For fear of any tumult that might arise to prevent the burning, Lord Williams and the householders of the city were commanded by the Queen's letter to be assistant, sufficiently armed; and when all things were in readiness, the prisoners were brought forth together, on the 16th of October, 1555.

"Ridley came first, in a furred black gown, such as he was wont to wear as a Bishop. After him came Latimer, in a poor Bristol frieze frock, all worn, with his buttoned cap and kerchief over his head, and a long new shroud hanging over his hose, down to his feet.

"Ridley, looking back, saw Latimer coming after, to whom he said, 'Oh be ye there?' 'Yea!' said Master Latimer, 'as fast as I can follow.' At length they came to the stake one after the other. Ridley first entered the place, and earnestly holding up both his hands, looked towards heaven. Shortly after, seeing Latimer, he ran to him, embraced and kissed him, saying, 'Be of good cheer, brother, for God will either assuage the fury of the flames or else strengthen us to abide it.'

"With that he went to the stake, kneeled down by it, kissed it, and prayed; and behind him Latimer kneeled, earnestly calling upon God. After they arose, the one talked with the other a little while, but what they said Foxe could not learn of any man.

"Then they were compelled to listen to a sermon preached by a renegade priest, named Smith, upon the text, 'Though I give my body to be burned, and have not charity, I am nothing.' They attempted to answer the false statements of this miserable discourse, but were not allowed. Ridley said, 'Well, then, I commit our cause to Almighty God, who shall impartially judge all.' Latimer added his own verse: 'Well, there is nothing hid but it shall be made manifest;' and said he could answer Smith well enough, if he might be suffered.

"They were commanded after this to make ready immediately, and obeyed with all meekness. Ridley gave his clothes and such things as he had about him to those that stood by, and happy was he that could get any rag of him. Latimer gave nothing, but quietly suffered his keeper to pull off his hose and his other apparel, which was very simple. And now being stripped to his shroud, he seemed as comely a person to them that stood by as one could desire to see. And though in his clothes he appeared a withered, crooked old man, he now stood bolt upright.

"Then the smith took a chain of iron and fastened it about both Ridley's and Latimer's middles to one stake. As he was knocking in a staple, Ridley took the chain in his hands, and said to the smith, 'Good fellow, knock it in hard, for flesh will have its course.' A bag of gunpowder was tied about the neck of each. Faggots were piled around them, and the horrible preparations were completed.

"Then they brought a faggot kindled with fire, and laid it down at Ridley's feet, to whom Latimer then spake in this manner: 'BE OF GOOD COMFORT, MASTER RIDLEY, AND PLAY THE MAN; WE SHALL THIS DAY LIGHT SUCH A CANDLE, BY GOD'S GRACE, IN ENGLAND, AS I TRUST SHALL NEVER BE PUT OUT.'

"And so the fire being kindled, when Ridley saw the fire flaming up towards him, he cried with a loud voice, 'Lord, into Thy hands I commend my spirit: Lord, receive my spirit!' and repeated the latter part often. Latimer, crying as vehemently on the other side of the stake, 'Father of heaven, receive my soul!' received the flame as if embracing it. After he had stroked his face with his hands, and as it were bathed them a little in the fire, he soon died, as it appeared, with very little pain."

"And thus much," says Foxe, "concerning the end of this old blessed servant of God, Bishop Latimer, for whose laborious services, fruitful life, and constant death, the whole realm has cause to give great thanks to Almighty God."

Latimer lived and died unmarried, and I am not aware that any English family at this day lays claim to any connection with him. But he left behind him a name far better than that of sons and daughters, a name which will be held in honour by all true English Protestants, so long as the world stands.

'Of all the Marian martyrs," says Fuller, "Mr Philpot was the best-born gentleman, Bishop Ridley the profoundest scholar, Mr Bradford the holiest and devoutest man, Archbishop Cranmer of the mildest and meekest temper, Bishop Hooper of the sternest and austerest nature, Dr Taylor had the merriest and pleasantest wit, but Mr Latimer had the plainest and simplest heart."

III. I turn from the subject of Latimer's life to *his opinions*. I have given a brief sketch of his history, from his birth to his death. My readers will easily believe that I have left many things untold.

I might dwell on the good man's *preaching*. Few, probably have ever addressed an English congregation with more effect than he did. No doubt his sermons now extant would not suit modern taste. They contain many quaint, odd, and coarse things. They are very familiar, rambling, and discursive, and often full of gossiping stories. But, after all, we are poor judges in these days of what a sermon ought to be. A modern sermon is too often a dull, tame, pointless religious essay, full of measured, round sentences, Johnsonian English, bald platitudes, timid statements, and elaborately concocted milk and water. It is a leaden sword, without either point or edge: a heavy weapon, and little likely to do much execution. But if a combination of sound Gospel doctrine, plain Saxon language, boldness, liveliness, directness, and simplicity, can make a preacher, few, I suspect, have ever equalled old Latimer.

I might supply many proofs of his *courage and faithfulness as a minister*. He did not shrink from attacking anybody's sins, even if they were the sins of a King. When Henry VIII checked the diffusion of the Bible, Latimer wrote him a plain-spoken letter, long before he was a Bishop, remonstrating with him on his conduct. He feared God, and nothing else did he fear. "Latimer, Latimer," he exclaimed at the beginning of one of his sermons, "thou art going to speak before the high and mighty King Henry VIII, who is able, if he think fit, to take thy life away. Be careful what thou sayest. But Latimer, Latimer, remember also thou art about to speak before the King of kings, and Lord of lords. Take heed that thou dost not displease Him."

I might speak of his *unworldliness*. He gave up a rich Bishopric, and retired into private life, for conscience' sake, without a murmur. He refused that same Bishopric again, because he felt too old to fulfil his duties, when he might have had it by saying "Yes." I might speak of his *genuine kindliness* of heart. He was always the friend of the poor and distressed. Much of his time, while he stayed at Lambeth, was occupied in examining into the cases of people who applied to him for help. I might speak of his *diligence*. To the very end of his life he used to rise at two o'clock in the morning, and begin reading and study. All this, and much more, I might tell, if I entered into more particulars in this biography.

I trust, however, I have given facts enough to supply some faint idea of what the man was. I trust my readers will agree with me, that he was one of the best Bishops this country has ever had, and that it would have been well for the Church of England if more of her Bishops had been like Bishop Latimer.

Let us never forget, as we think over the history of his life, that he is a glorious instance of the miracles which the grace of God can work. The Holy Spirit can take a bigoted, fierce Papist and make him a faithful Protestant. Where the hand of the Lord is, nothing is impossible. Let us never think that any friend, relative, or companion is too much opposed to the Gospel to become a true Christian. Away with the idea! There are no hopeless cases under the Gospel. Let us remember Latimer, and never despair.

From all these topics, however interesting, I turn to one which is even more important in the present day. That topic is, the nature of Latimer's theological opinions. For dwelling on this topic at some length I shall make no apology. The circumstances of the times we live in invest the subject with more than ordinary importance.

We live in days when very strange statements are made in some quarters, as to the true doctrines of the Church of England. Semi-Popish views about the rule of faith, about justification, about regeneration, about the sacraments, about preaching, are continually urged upon the attention of congregations, while the advocates and teachers of these views are coolly arrogating to themselves the credit of being the only sound Churchmen.

It is to no purpose that those who repudiate these semi-Popish views challenge their advocates to prove them by Scripture. The ready answer is at once given, that, whether these views are Scriptural or not, there can be no doubt they are "*Church views.*" It is to no purpose that we deny these views are to be found in the Articles, Liturgy, and Homilies of the Church of England, when honestly and consistently interpreted. We are quietly told that we know nothing about the matter. We are stupid! We are blind! We are ignorant! We do not understand plain English! They are the true men! Their views are the true "Church views," and if we disagree with them, we must be quite wrong! In short, we are left to infer that, if we are honest and consistent, we ought to leave our dear old Church, and give it up to the extreme Ritualists. I appeal to the experience of every one who lives with his eyes open and marks the signs of the times. My readers know well I am describing things which are going on in every part of the land.

Now, as matters have come to this pass, let us throw a little light on the subject by looking back 300 years. Let us inquire what were the views of the men who laid the foundations of the Church of England, and are notoriously the fathers of the Articles, Homilies, and Liturgy. Let us put old Latimer into the witness-box to-day, and see what his opinions were upon the points in dispute. An honoured member of the Church of England, at the period when the doctrines of the Church were first brought into shape and form, a near and dear friend and adviser of Archbishop Cranmer, an assistant in the composition of the first book of Homilies, a Bishop whose orthodoxy and soundness were never called in question for a moment by his contemporaries, if any man knows what a true Churchman ought to hold, Bishop Latimer must surely be that man. If his views are not true "Church" views, I know not whose are.

I ask my readers, then, to bear with me for a few minutes, while I give some extracts from Latimer's works. Quotations from old writers, I am well aware, are very wearisome, and seldom read. But I want to inform the minds of Englishmen on the important question of the present day, Who is, and who is not a true Churchman?

(1) First of all, what did Bishop Latimer think about SCRIPTURE? This is a point with which the very existence of true religion is bound up. Some Churchmen tell us nowadays, notwithstanding the Sixth Article, that the Bible alone is not the rule of faith, and is not able to make a man wise unto salvation. No! it must be the Bible and the Fathers, or the Bible and Catholic tradition, or the Bible and the Church, or the Bible explained by the Prayer-book, or the Bible explained by an episcopally-ordained man, but not the Bible alone. Now let us hear Bishop Latimer.

He says, in a sermon before Edward VI, "I will tell you what a Bishop of this realm once said to me. He sent for me and marvelled that I would not consent to such traditions as were then set out. And I answered him, that I would be ruled by God's Book, and rather than depart one jot from it I would be torn by wild horses. I chanced in our communication to name the Lord's Supper. Tush! saith the Bishop. What do you call the Lord's Supper? What new term is this? There stood by him one Dr Dubber. He dubbed him by-and-by, and said that this term was seldom read in the doctors. And I made answer, that I would rather follow Paul in using his terms than them, though they had all the doctors on their side." (Works, i. 121.)

He says again, in his conference with Ridley: "A layman, fearing God, is much more fit to understand holy Scripture than any arrogant or proud priest; yea, than the Bishop himself, be he never so great and glistering in all his pontificals. But what is to be said of the Fathers? How are they to be esteemed? St Augustine answereth, giving this rule, that we should not therefore think it true because they say so, do they never so much excel in holiness or learning; but if they be able to prove their saying by canonical Scripture, or by good probable reason; meaning that to be a probable reason, I think, which doth orderly follow upon a right collection and gathering out of the Scriptures.

"Let the Papists go with their long faith. Be you contented with the short faith of the saints, which is revealed to us in the Word of God written. Adieu to all Popish fantasies. Amen! For one man having the Scripture, and good reason for him, is more to be esteemed himself alone, than a thousand such as they, either gathered together, or succeeding one another. The Fathers have both herbs and weeds, and Papists commonly gather the weeds, and leave the herbs." (Ridley's Works, p. 114. Parker Society edition.)

I make no comment on these passages, they speak for themselves.

(2) In the next place, what did Bishop Latimer think about *justification by faith*? This is the doctrine which Luther truly called the criterion of a standing or falling Church. This is the doctrine which, in spite of the Eleventh Article of our Church, many are now trying to obscure, by mingling up with it baptism, the Lord's

Supper, our own works, and I know not what besides. Now let us hear Bishop Latimer.

He says, in a sermon, preached at Grimsthorpe, Lincolnshire, "Christ reputeth all those for just, holy, and acceptable before God, which believe in Him, which put their trust, hope and confidence in Him. By His passion which He suffered, He merited that as many as believe in Him shall be as well justified by Him as though they themselves had never done any sin, and as though they had fulfilled the law to the uttermost. For we without Him are under the curse of the law. The law condemneth us. The law is not able to help us. And yet the imperfection is not in the law, but in us. The law itself is holy and good, but we are not able to keep it, and so the law condemneth us. But Christ with His death hath delivered us from the curse of the law. He hath set us at liberty, and promised that when we believe in Him we shall not perish, the law shall not condemn us. Therefore let us study to believe in Christ. Let us put all our hope, trust, and confidence only in Him. Let us patch Him with nothing, for, as I told you before, our merits are not able to deserve everlasting life. It is too precious a thing to be merited by man. It is His doing only. God hath given Him to us to be our Deliverer, and to give us everlasting life." (ii. 125.)

He says again, in another sermon, "Learn to abhor the most detestable and dangerous poison of the Papists, which go about to thrust Christ out of His office. Learn, I say, to leave all Papistry, and to stick only to the Word of God, which teacheth that Christ is not only a judge but a justifier, a giver of salvation, and a taker away of sin. He purchased our salvation through His painful death, and we receive the same through believing in Him, as St Paul teacheth us, saying, Freely ye are justified through faith. In these words of St Paul, all merits and estimation of works are excluded and clean taken away. For if it were for our works' sake, then it were not freely, but St Paul saith *freely*. Whether will you now believe St Paul or the Papists?" (ii. 147.)

He says again, in another sermon: "Christ only, and no man else, merited remission, justification, and eternal felicity, for as many as will believe the same. They that will not believe it, shall not have it; for it is no more but, Believe and have." (i. 521.)

Once more I say, these passages require no comment of mine. They speak for themselves.

(3) In the next place, what did Bishop Latimer think about *regeneration*? This, as you are all aware, is the subject of one of the great controversies of the day. Multitudes of Churchmen, in spite of the Seventeenth Article, and the Homily for Whit Sunday, maintain that all baptized persons are necessarily regenerate, and receive grace and the Holy Ghost at the moment they are baptized. In a word, they tell us that every man, woman, and child, who has received baptism, has also received regeneration, and that every congregation in the Church of England should be addressed as an assembly of regenerated persons. Now let us hear Bishop Latimer.

He says, in a sermon preached in Lincolnshire, "There be two manner of men. Some there be that be not justified, not regenerate, not yet in the state of salvation, that is to say, not God's servants. They lack the renovation, or regeneration. They be not yet come to Christ." (ii. 7.) He says, in a sermon preached before Edward VI, "Christ saith, Except a man be born from above, he cannot see the kingdom of God. He must have a regeneration. And what is this regeneration? *It is not to be christened in water*, as these firebrands expound it, and nothing else. How is it to be expounded, then? St Peter showeth that one place of Scripture declareth another. It is the circumstance and collation of places that maketh Scripture plain. We be born again, says Peter, and how? Not by a mortal seed, but an immortal. What is this immortal seed? By the Word of the living God: by the Word of God preached and opened. Thus cometh in our new birth." (i. 202.) He says, in another Lincolnshire sermon, "Preaching is God's instrument, whereby He worketh faith in our hearts. Our Saviour saith to Nicodemus, Except a man be born anew, he cannot see the kingdom of God. But how cometh this regeneration? By hearing and believing the Word of God: for so saith St Peter." (i. 471.)

Once more I say, these passages require no comment of mine. They speak for themselves.

(4) In the next place, what did Bishop Latimer think about the *Lord's Supper*? This, I need hardly say, is a subject about which very unprotestant doctrine is often taught in the present day. Some around us, in the face of the Twenty-eighth Article, speak

of this sacrament in such a manner, that it is hard to see the difference between their doctrine and Popish transubstantiation or the sacrifice of the Mass. Now let us hear Bishop Latimer.

He says, in his disputation at Oxford, "[In the sacrament] there is none other presence of Christ required than a spiritual presence. And this presence is sufficient for a Christian man, as the presence by the which we both abide in Christ, and Christ in us, to the obtaining of eternal life, if we persevere in his true Gospel. And the same presence may be called a real presence, because to the faithful believer there is the real or spiritual body of Christ." (ii. 252.) He says, in the same disputation, "Christ spake never a word of sacrificing, or saying of Mass; nor promised the hearers any reward, but among the idolators with the devil and his angels, except they repent speedily with tears. Therefore, sacrificing priests should now cease for ever: for now all men ought to offer their own bodies a quick sacrifice, holy and acceptable before God. The Supper of the Lord was instituted to provoke us to thanksgiving, and to stir us up by preaching of the Gospel to remember His death till He cometh again." (ii. 255.) He says, in his last examination, "There is a change in the bread and wine, and such a change as no power but the omnipotency of God can make, in that that which before was bread should now have the dignity to exhibit Christ's body. And yet the bread is still bread, and the wine is still wine. For the change is *not in the nature but in the dignity*." (ii. 286.) He says, in one of his Lincolnshire sermons, "Whosoever eateth the mystical bread, and drinketh the mystical wine worthily, according to the ordinance of Christ, he receiveth surely the very body and blood of Christ spiritually, as it shall be most comfortable to his soul. He eateth with the mouth of his soul, and digesteth with the stomach of his soul, the body of Christ. And to be short, whosoever believeth in Christ, putteth his hope, trust, and confidence in Him, he eateth and drinketh Him. For the spiritual eating is the right eating to everlasting life, not the corporal eating." (i. 458.)

Once more I say, I make no comment on these passages. They speak for themselves.

It would be easy to multiply quotations of this kind to an endless length, if it were necessary or desirable. There is hardly a controverted subject in the present day on which I could not give some plain, Scriptural, sensible, sound opinion of Bishop Latimer.

Would my readers like to know what he thought about the ordinance of *preaching*? Did he think little of it, as some do in this day; and regard it as a means of grace very subordinate to sacraments and services? No, indeed he did not! He calls it "the office of salvation, and the office of regeneration." He says, "Take away preaching, and take away salvation." He says, "This office of preaching is the only ordinary way that God hath appointed to save us all by. Let us maintain this, for I know no other." He declares that "preaching is the thing the devil wrestled most against. It has been all his study to decry this office. He worketh against it as much as he can. He hath made unpreaching prelates, and stirred them up by heaps to persecute this office in the title of heresy." (i. 203, 155, 306.)

Would my readers like to hear what he thought about a *gorgeous ceremonial and candles in Churches*? He says plainly that these things come from the devil. "Where the devil is resident, and hath his plough going, there away with books and up with candles; away with the Bibles and up with beads; away with the light of the Gospel and up with the light of candles, yea, even at noonday. Where the devil is resident, that he may prevail, up with all superstition and idolatry, censing, painting of images, candles, palms, ashes, holy water, and new service of men's inventing." (i. 70.)

Would my readers like to know what he thought about the *foreign reformers*? Did he lightly esteem them, as some do nowadays, because they did not retain episcopacy? No, indeed he did not! He says, "I heard say, Melanchthon, that great clerk, should come hither. I would wish him, and such as he is, to have £200 a-year. The King would never want it. There are yet among us two great learned men, Peter Martyr and Bernard Ochin, which have a hundred marks a-piece. I would the King would bestow a thousand pounds on that sort." (i. 141.)

Would my readers like to know what he thought about *unity*? Did he think, as some do now, that it is the one thing needful, and that we should give up every thing in order to attain it? No, indeed! He said, "Unity must be according to God's Holy Word, or else it were better war than peace. We ought never to regard unity so much that we forsake God's Word for her sake." (i. 487.)

Would my readers like to know what he thought about *councils and convocations*? Did he regard them as the grand panacea for all ecclesiastical evils, like those around us, whose cry is, "Give us synodical action, or we die"? He says to Ridley, "Touching councils and convocations, I refer you to your own experience, to think of our own country's parliaments and convocations. The more part in my time did bring forth the Six Articles. Afterward the more part did repeal the same. The same Articles are now again restored. Oh, what uncertainty is this!" And he says, in another place, "More credence is to be given to one man having the Holy Word of God for him, than to ten thousand without the Word. If it agrees with God's Word, it is to be received. If it agrees not, it is not to be received, though a council had determined it." (Ridley, 130; Latim. i. 288.)

Would my readers like to know what he thought of *thorough-going Protestant preaching*? Did he think, as some do now, that if a sermon contains a good deal of truth, a little false doctrine may be excused and allowed? No, indeed he did not! He says, "Many teach God's way, and shall preach a very good and godly sermon, but at the last they will have a blanched almond, one little piece of Popery patched in to powder their matter with, for their own lucre and glory. They make a mingling of the way of God and man's way, a mingle-mangle, as men serve pigs in my country." (i. 290.)

I will not multiply these extracts, though it would be easy to do so. Those who have never studied the works of Latimer, published by the Parker Society, have little idea of the loss they have sustained. They are rich to overflowing with pithy, pointed Protestant truths. I will only ask my readers to remember well those words I have been quoting, and when they were spoken.

These words were not spoken last year. They did not fall from the lips of modern Evangelical or Low Church clergymen. No: the words I have quoted are more than 300 years old. They are the words of one of the best Bishops the Church of England ever had. They are the words of the man who helped to compose our first book of Homilies. They are the words of the friend and adviser of Archbishop Cranmer. They are the words of one whom King and Parliament delighted to honour.

Why was the speaker of these words not cast out of the Church of England? Why was he not reprimanded? Why was he not reviled as a man of low, unchurchmanlike opinions? Why was he not proceeded against and persecuted for his views? How is it that he was persecuted only by Papists, but always honoured by Protestants? persecuted by Bonner, Gardiner, and Bloody Mary; but honoured by Cranmer, Ridley, and Edward VI?

I will give a plain answer to these questions. I answer them by saying that, at the time of which I write, no man in his senses doubted that Latimer's opinions were the real opinions of the Church of England. I go on further to affirm that the truest and best members of the Church of England, at the present day, are those whose views are most in harmony with those of good Bishop Latimer. And I say, that to tell men who love the Church of England with deep affection, that they are not sound Churchmen, merely because they agree with Latimer, and not with Laud, is to bring against them a most unfair and unwarrantable charge.

And now let me conclude this biography of Latimer with two practical remarks.

(a) For one thing, let me earnestly exhort my readers, as individuals, *never to be ashamed of holding what are called Evangelical views within the Church of England.* Listen not to those supercilious gentlemen, on the one side, who would have you believe that if you are not High Churchmen like themselves, you are no Churchmen at all. Listen not to those exceedingly kind friends, on the other side, who try to persuade you that the Established Church maintains Popish doctrines, and ought to be left at once. Both these are ancient tricks. Against both these tricks be on your guard.

Do not be bullied out of the Church of England by the High Churchman's assertion that you are only a tolerated party, and have no business by his side. No doubt you live in a communion where great freedom of opinion is allowed. But to tell men of Evangelical views that they are merely *tolerated*, is a downright insult to the memory of the Reformers. Let us make answer to people who tell us so, that if they have forgotten Latimer and three hundred years ago, we have not. Let us say that we are not going to desert the Church of Latimer, in order to please men who wish to lord it over God's heritage, and have things all their own way. Sure I am that if might should ever prevail over right, and the friends of Latimer should be thrust out of the Church by force, and the House of Commons should be mad enough to sanction it, sure am I that the men thrust out would be better Churchmen than the men left behind.

And do not be wheedled out of the Church by the arguments of men outside, who would probably be glad to be in it if they only saw the way. When the fox, in an old fable, could not reach the grapes, he said they were sour. When the fox, in another fable, lost his tail in a trap, he tried to persuade his friends that foxes did much better without tails, and advised them to get rid of their own. Do not forget the moral of that fable; do not be enticed into biting off your own tails. Rest assured, that with all its faults and defects the Church of England has very high privileges to offer to its members. Think well about these privileges. Do not be always poring over the defects. Resolve that you will not lightly cast these privileges away.

Above all, never, never forget that Evangelical views are not only theoretically sound, and agreeable to the mind of the Reformers, but that they are also of vital importance to the very existence of the Church of England. Never has our beloved Church stood so low in this country as when Evangelical views have been at zero, and almost forgotten. Never has she stood so high as when the views of Latimer and the Reformers have been honestly preached and carried out. So far from being ashamed of Evangelical opinions, you may be satisfied that the maintenance of them is rapidly becoming a matter of life or death to your own communion. Take away Latimer's views, and I firmly believe the whole Establishment would collapse before the pressure from without, and come to the ground.

(*b*) For another thing, let me entreat all English readers of this biography to *beware of countenancing any retrograde movement in this country towards the Church of Rome, and to resist such movement by every possible means, from whatever quarter it may come.*

I am sure that this warning is one which the times loudly call for. The Church of Rome has risen up amongst us with renewed strength in the last few years. She does not disguise her hope that England, the lost planet, will soon resume her orbit in the so-called Catholic system, and once more revolve in blind obedience round the centre of the Vatican. She has succeeded in blinding the eyes of ignorant persons to her real character. She has succeeded in securing the unexpected aid of misguided men within our own Establishment. A hundred little symptoms around us tell us how real the danger is. Laud and the nonjurors are cried up, while Latimer and the Reformers are cried down. Historical works are industriously circulated, in which Bloody Mary is praised, and Protestant Elizabeth blamed. A morbid tenderness towards Romanists, and a virulent bitterness towards Dissenters have sprung up side by side. An unhealthy attention is paid to what is called mediæval taste. Thousands of tracts are sown broad-cast over the land in which are generally these three ominous words, "*priest*," "*catholic*," and "*church*." The use of the rosary, auricular confession, prayers for the dead, and the "Hail, Mary," are deliberately recommended to the members of the English Church. Little by little, I fear, the edge of English feeling about Popery is becoming blunt and dull. Surely I have good reason to tell my readers to beware of the Church of Rome.

Remember the darkness in which Rome kept England when she last had the supreme power. Remember the gross ignorance and degrading superstitions which prevailed in Bishop Latimer's youth. Think not for a moment that these are ancient things, and that Rome is changed. The holy coat of Trèves, the winking picture at Rimini, the mental thraldom in which the Papal States have been kept, the notorious practices which go on in the Holy City to this day, are all witnesses that Rome, when she has the power, is not changed at all. Remember this, and beware.

Remember the horrible persecutions which Rome carried on against true religion, when she last had uncontrolled sway in this country. Remember the atrocities which disgraced the days of Bloody Mary, and the burning of Bishop Latimer. Think not for a moment that Rome is altered. The persecution of Bible readers in Madeira, and the imprisonment of the Madiai, are unmistakable proof that, after three hundred years, the old persecuting spirit of Rome still remains as strong as ever. Remember this also, and beware.

Shall we, in the face of such facts as these, return to the bondage in which our forefathers were kept? Shall we give up our Bibles, or be content to sue for sacerdotal licence to read them? Shall we submit ourselves humbly to Italian priests? Shall we go back to confessional-boxes and the idolatrous sacrifice of the Mass. God forbid! I say for one—God fobid! Let the dog return to his vomit. Let the sow that was washed return to her wallowing in the mire. Let the idiotic prisoner go back to his chains. But God forbid that Israel should return to Egypt! God forbid that England should go back into the arms of Rome! God forbid that old Latimer's candle should ever be put out!

Let us work, every one of us, if we would prevent such a miserable consummation. Let us work hard for the extension of pure, Scriptural, and Evangelical religion at home and abroad. Let us labour to spread it among the Jews, among the Roman Catholics, among the heathen. Let us labour not least to preserve and maintain it by every constitutional means in our own Church.

Let us cherish, every one of us, if we would prevent the increase of Romanism, a brotherly feeling towards all orthodox Protestants, by whatever name they may be called. Away with the old rubbishy opinion, that the Church of England occupies a middle position, a *via media*, between Dissent and Rome. Cast it away, for it is false. We might as well talk of the Isle of Wight being midway between England and France. Between us and Rome there is a gulf, and a broad and deep gulf too. Between us and orthodox Protestant Dissent there is but a thin partition wall. Between us and Rome the differences are about essential doctrines, and things absolutely necessary to salvation. Between us and Dissent the division is about things indifferent, things in which a man may err, and yet be saved. Rome is a downright open enemy, attacking the very foundation of our religion. Dissent ought to be an ally and friendly power; not wearing our uniform, nor yet, as we think, so well equipped as we are, but still an ally, and fighting on the same side. Let not this hint be thrown away! Let us keep up a kind, brotherly feeling towards all who love the same Saviour, believe the same doctrines, and honour the same Bible as ourselves.

Finally, let us pray, every one of us, if we would prevent the increase of Romanism, let us pray night and day that God may preserve this country from Popery, and not deal with it according to its sins. It is a striking fact, that almost the last prayer of good King Edward VI, on his death-bed, was a prayer to this effect: "O my Lord God, defend this realm from Papistry, and maintain Thy true religion." There was a prayer in the Litany of our Prayer-book, in 1549, which many think never ought to have been cast out of it: "From all sedition, and privy conspiracy, FROM THE TYRANNY OF THE BISHOP OF ROME, AND ALL HIS DETESTABLE ENORMITIES, from all false doctrine and heresy, from hardness of heart, and contempt of Thy Word and commandments, good Lord, deliver us!' To that prayer may we ever be able to say heartily, Amen, and Amen!

JOHN BRADFORD: MARTYR

John Bradford, the famous English Reformer, who was burned at Smithfield for Christ's truth, in Queen Mary's days, is far better known as a martyr than as a writer. The splendour of his death has eclipsed the work of his pen. Few perhaps have the least idea what a rich treasure of English theology is laid up in his literary remains.

This ought not so to be. Among the many goodly volumes published by the Parker Society, not a few, I suspect, sleep quietly on library shelves, unopened and uncut. Like ancient weapons of war, they are too ponderous for the taste of our day. Like guns and shells in Woolwich Arsenal, they are regarded as stores to be used only in special times of need. Yet some of these volumes will richly repay an attentive perusal. Latimer, Hooper, and Jewell should never be neglected. Side-by-side with these three men I am disposed to rank the two volumes of Bradford's writings, from which I propose to make some selections at the conclusion of this chapter.

Some account of Bradford's life and death will prove a suitable preface to the extracts I shall give from his writings. It is to many an old story, and well known; yet in days like these it is well to stir up men's minds by putting them in remembrance of the champions of the English Reformation. For a large portion of the information I give, I am indebted to a biography of Bradford, written by the Rev. Aubrey Townsend, and prefixed to the Parker Society's edition of Bradford's works.

John Bradford, Prebendary of St Paul's and Chaplain to Bishop Ridley, was born at Blackley, near Manchester, about the year

[1] The two volumes *Writings of John Bradford* were issued by the Parker Society, 1848 and 1853. They are currently reprinted by the Banner of Truth Trust, 1979.

1510. Foxe records that he was "brought up in virtue and good learning even from his very childhood and, among other praises of his good education, he obtained as a chief gift the cunning and readiness of writing, which knowledge was not only an ornament unto him, but also an help to the necessary sustentation of his living." Baines, the historian of the county of Lancaster, also observes that Bradford, having received a liberal education at the free grammar school in Manchester, founded by Bishop Oldham, who died in 1519, attained there a considerable proficiency in Latin and arithmetic.

"To this early period of his life Bradford, writing from prison in the days of Mary, feelingly adverts:

'I cannot but say that I have most cause to thank Thee for my parents, schoolmasters, and others, under whose tuition Thou hast put me. No pen is able to write the particular benefits, which I have already received in my infancy, childhood, youth, middle age, and always hitherto. . . . I could reckon innumerable behind me, and but few before me, so much made of and cared for as I have been hitherto.'

"Foxe records that Bradford, at a later period, 'became servant to Sir John Harrington, Knight, of Exton, in Rutlandshire, who, in the great affairs of Henry VIII, and King Edward VI, which he had in hand when he was treasurer of the King's camps and buildings, at divers times, in Boulogne, had such experience of Bradford's activity in writing, of his expertness in the art of auditors, and also of his faithful trustiness, that, not only in those affairs, but in many other of his private business, he trusted Bradford in such sort, that above all others he used his faithful service.' At the siege of Montreuil in particular, conducted by the English under the Duke of Norfolk in the year 1544, Bradford discharged, under Sir John Harrington, the office of paymaster.

"Three years later, not long after the accession of Edward VI, on the 8th April, 1547, Bradford entered the Inner Temple as a student of common law. His character then underwent a complete change. Twenty-seven years later, Sampson, his friend and fellow-student at the Temple, and who, it has been said, was the human means, under a higher power, of that great transformation, writes, in his preface to Bradford's works: 'I did know when, and partly how, it pleased God, by effectual calling, to turn his heart unto the true knowledge and obedience of the most holy Gospel of Christ our Saviour; of which God did give him such an heavenly hold and lively feeling, that, as he did then know that many sins were forgiven him, so surely he declared by deeds that he 'loved much.' For, where he had both gifts and calling to have employed himself in civil and worldly affairs profitably, such was his love of Christ and zeal to the promoting of His glorious Gospel, that he changed not only the course of his former life, as the woman did (Luke vii.), but even his former study, as Paul did change his former profession and study.

" 'Touching the first, after that God touched his heart with that holy and effectual calling, he sold his chains, rings, brooches and jewels of gold, which before he used to wear, and did bestow the price of this his former vanity in the necessary relief of Christ's poor members, which he could hear of or find lying sick or pining in poverty. Touching the second, he so declared his great zeal and love to promote the glory of the Lord Jesus, whose goodness and saving health he had tasted, that,' 'with marvellous favour to further the kingdom of God by the ministry of His Holy Word, he gave himself wholly to the study of the Holy Scriptures. The which his purpose to accomplish the better, he departed from the Temple at London, where the temporal law is studied, and went to the University of Cambridge, to learn, by God's law, how to further the building of the Lord's temple.'

"An incident occurred, while he was in London, which occasioned him deep anxiety. He 'heard a sermon which that notable preacher, Master Latimer, made before King Edward VI, in which he did earnestly speak of restitution to be made of things falsely gotten.' This 'did so strike him to the heart' on account of a fraud, committed by his master, Sir John Harrington, which 'was to the deceiving of the King,' and which it would seem Bradford had concealed, 'that he could never be quiet till by the advice of the same Master Latimer a restitution was made.' That he had not been an interested party to this fraud would appear from his words to Bishop Gardiner, January 30th, 1555: 'My lord, I set my foot to his foot, whosoever he be, that can come forth, and justly vouch to my face that ever I deceived my master: and, as you are chief justice by office in England, I desire justice upon them that so slander me, because they cannot prove it.' This was a challenge, which he could scarcely have ventured to make, if he had himself defrauded the government. It was through his firmness, in fact, that Sir John Harrington was compelled to make restitution to the King of the sums falsely obtained, in the two successive years, 1549 and 1550."

In the year 1548 Bradford became a student at Cambridge, first at Catharine Hall, and afterwards at Pembroke Hall, where he became a Fellow. His letter describing his Fellowship is curious and interesting. " 'I am now a Fellow of Pembroke Hall, of the which I nor any other for me did ever make any suit; yea, there was a contention betwixt the Master of Catharine's Hall (Sandys) and the Bishop of Rochester, who is Master of Pembroke Hall, whether should have me. . . . My Fellowship here is worth seven pounds a year; for I have allowed me eighteen-pence a week, and as good as thirty-three shillings four pence a year in money, besides my chamber, launder, barber, &c.; and I am bound to nothing but once or twice a year to keep a problem. Thus you see what a good Lord God is unto me.'

"His friend Sampson graphically depicts Bradford's holy walk with God at this period: 'His manner was, to make to himself a catalogue of all the grossest and most enorme sins, which in his life of ignorance he had committed; and to lay the same before his eyes when he went to private prayer, that by the sight and remembrance of them he might be stirred up to offer to God the sacrifice of a contrite heart, seek assurance of salvation in Christ by faith, thank God for his calling from the ways of wickedness, and pray for increase of grace to be conducted in holy life acceptable and pleasing to God. Such a continual exercise of conscience he had in private prayer, that he did not count himself to have prayed to his contentation, unless in it he had felt inwardly some smiting of heart for sin, and some healing of that wound by faith, feeling the saving health of Christ, with some change of mind into the detestation of sin, and love of obeying the good will of God. . . . Without such an inward exercise of prayer our Bradford did not pray to his full contentation, as appeared by this: he used in the morning to go to the common prayer in the college where he was, and after that he used to make some prayer with his pupils in his chamber: but not content with this, he then repaired to his own secret prayer and exercise in prayer by himself, as one that had not yet prayed to his own mind; for he was wont to say to his familiars, "I have prayed with my pupils, but I have not yet prayed with myself."

"Another of his exercises was this: he used to make unto himself an ephemeris or a journal, in which he used to write all such notable things as either he did see or hear each day that passed. But, whatsoever he did hear or see, he did so pen it that a man might see in that book the signs of his smitten heart. For, if he did see or hear any good in any man, by that sight he found and noted the want thereof in himself, and added a short prayer, craving mercy and grace to amend. If he did hear or see any plague or misery, he noted it as a thing procured by his own sins, and still added, *Domine miserere mei*, "Lord, have mercy upon me." He used in the same book to note such evil thoughts as did rise in him; as of envying the good of other men, thoughts of unthankfulness, of not considering God in his works, of hardness and unsensibleness of heart when he did see other moved and affected. And thus he made to himself and of himself a book of daily practices of repentance."

At Cambridge, Bradford became intimate with Bucer, Sandys, and Ridley, and was tutor to Whitgift, afterwards Archbishop of Canterbury. He was ordained by Ridley in 1550, and strongly recommended to King Edward VI, on account of his high talents and piety. Shortly afterwards, by Ridley's advice, the King appointed him to be one of the six royal chaplains who were sent about England, with a kind of roving commission, to preach up the doctrines of the Reformation. Bradford's commission was to preach in Lancashire and Cheshire, being connected with those counties; and he seems to have performed his duty with singular ability and success. He preached constantly in Manchester, Liverpool, Bolton, Bury, Wigan, Ashton, Stockport, Eccles, Middleton, and Chester, with great benefit to the cause of Protestantism, and with great effect on men's souls.

"At the close of 1552, when Bradford was at Manchester, he 'treated of Noe's flood,' and often forewarned the people of 'those plagues' which would be 'brought to pass.' And on the twenty-sixth of December, St Stephen's Day, 'the last time that he was with them,' he preached a remarkable sermon from the twenty-third chapter of St Matthew. The last six verses, the gospel for the day, was the text, no doubt, he selected on that occasion, a passage eminently suggestive of that solemn and prophetic warning which he then delivered. Local tradition even yet points to the spot in Blackley, where the country people say that Bradford, during that last visit to Manchester, knelt down and made solemn supplication to Almighty God. His request at the throne of grace was that the everlasting Gospel might be preached in Blackley, to the end of time, by ministers divinely taught to feed the flock with wisdom and knowledge. The martyr's prayer, it is alleged, has been answered in the continuance, with scarcely an exception, of faithful men in that place.

"Sampson informs us, that 'besides often preaching in London and at Paul's Cross, and sundry places in the country, and especially in Lancashire, Bradford preached before King Edward VI, in the Lent, the last year of his reign, upon the second Psalm; and there in one sermon, showing the tokens of God's judgment at hand for the contempt of the Gospel, as that certain gentlemen upon the Sabbath Day going in a wherry to Paris Garden, to the bear-baiting, were drowned, and that a dog was met at Ludgate carrying a piece of a dead child in his mouth, he with a mighty and prophetical spirit said, "I summon you all, even every mother's child of you, to the judgment of God, for it is at hand:" as it followed shortly after in the death of King Edward.' This was, perhaps, the occasion which John Knox so well describes in his 'Godly Letter,' 1554: 'Master Bradford. . . . spared not the proudest, but boldly declared that God's vengeance shortly should strike those that then were in authority, because they loathed and abhorred the true Word of the everlasting God; and amongst many other willed them to take ensample by the late Duke of Somerset, who became so cold in hearing God's Word, that, the year before his last apprehension, he would go to visit his masons, and would not dingy[1] himself from his gallery to go to his hall for hearing of a sermon. "God punished him," said that godly preacher, "and that suddenly: and shall He spare you that be double more wicked? No, He shall not. Will ye, or will ye not, ye shall drink the cup of the Lord's wrath. *Judicium Domini, judicium Domini!* The judgment of the Lord, the judgment of the Lord!" lamentably cried he with a lamentable voice and weeping tears.'

[1] Dingy = trouble

"Bishop Ridley, writing from prison in the reign of Mary, speaking of Bradford, Latimer, Lever, and Knox, bears the strongest testimony to the boldness and faithfulness with which they addressed the courtiers of Edward: 'Their tongues were so sharp, they ripped in so deep in their galled backs, to have purged them, no doubt, of that filthy matter that was festered in their hearts of insatiable covetousness, of filthy carnality and voluptuousness, of intolerable ambition and pride, of ungodly loathsomeness to hear poor men's causes and to hear God's Word, that these men of all other these magistrates then could never abide.'

"Sampson represents forcibly Bradford's habits in private life:

" 'They which were familiar with him might see how he, being in their company, used to fall often into a sudden and deep meditation, in which he would sit with fixed countenance and spirit moved, yet speaking nothing a good space. And sometimes in this silent sitting plenty of tears should trickle down his cheeks: sometime he would sit in it and come out of it with a smiling countenance. Oftentimes have I sitten at dinner and supper with him, in the house of that godly harbourer of many preachers and servants of the Lord Jesus, I mean Master Elsyng, when, either by occasion of talk had, or some view of God's benefits present, or some inward cogitation and thought of his own, he hath fallen into these deep cogitations: and he would tell me in the end such discourses of them, that I did perceive that sometimes his tears trickled out of his eyes, as well for joy as for sorrow. Neither was he only such a practiser of repentance in himself, but a continual provoker of others thereunto, not only in public preaching, but also in private conference and company. For in all companies where he did come he would freely reprove any sin and misbehaviour which appeared in any person, especially swearers, filthy talkers, and Popish praters. Such never departed out of his company unreproved. And this he did with such a Divine grace and Christian majesty, that ever he stopped the mouths of the gainsayers. For he spoke with power and yet so sweetly, that they might see their evil to be evil and hurtful unto them, and understand that it was good indeed to the which he laboured to draw them in God.' "

The consequence of Bradford's zeal for the principle of the Reformation, as soon as Edward VI died, was precisely what might have been expected. Within a month of Queen Mary's accession he was put into prison, like Cranmer, Ridley, Latimer, and Hooper, and never left it until he was burned. His singular holiness, and his great reputation as a preacher, made him an object of great interest during his imprisonment, and immense efforts were made to reason him out of his Protestantism, and pervert him to the Romish Church. All these efforts, however, were in vain. As he lived, so he died.

Sentence of condemnation was passed, January 31, 1555. It was at first intended to deliver him forthwith to the Earl of Derby, to be conveyed into Lancashire, and there to be burned in the town of Manchester, where he was born. The original purpose was subsequently abandoned. The Romish bishops, whether from secret fear of Bradford's friends (for Bradford was in favour among his own people), or from some more secret confidence of overcoming his opinion, retained him at London for some months, assailing him during that time with frequent conferences and embassies. And it appears from some pages, first reprinted in the former volume of his works from his Examinations, that the Earl of Derby took great interest in his case, and (it was alleged) obtained from the Queen the concession, that he should "have his books, and time enough to peruse them."

On the day of Bradford's execution he was led out from Newgate to Smithfield about nine o'clock in the morning of July 1, 1555, amidst such a crowd of people as was never seen either before or after. A certain Mrs Honywood, who lived to the age of ninety-two, and died in 1620, often told her friends that she remembered going to see him burned, and her shoes being trodden off by the crowd, so that she had to walk barefoot to Ludgate Hill.

The account of his martyrdom, as described by Foxe, is so touching that I shall give it in the Martyrologist's own words. In the afternoon of June 30th, "Suddenly the keeper's wife came up, as one half amazed, and seeming much troubled, being almost windless, said, 'Oh Master Bradford, I come to bring you heavy news.'—'What is that?' said he. 'Marry,' quoth she, 'tomorrow you must be burned, and your chain is now a-buying, and soon you must go to Newgate.' With that Master Bradford put off his cap, and lifting up his eyes to heaven said, 'I thank God for it; I have looked for the same a long time, and therefore it cometh not now to me suddenly, but as a thing waited for every day and hour; the Lord make me worthy thereof:' and so, thanking her for her gentleness, he departed up into his chamber, and called his friend with him, who when he came thither, he went secretly himself alone a long time, and prayed. Which done, he came again to him that was in his chamber, and took him divers writings and papers, and showed him his mind in those things what he would have done; and, after they had spent the afternoon till night in many and sundry such things, at last came to him half a dozen of his friends more, with whom all the evening he spent the time in prayer and other good exercises, so wonderfully that it was marvellous to hear and see his doings.

"A little before he went out of the Compter, he made a notable prayer of his farewell, with such plenty of tears, and abundant spirit of prayer, that it ravished the minds of the hearers. Also when he shifted himself with a clean shirt, that was made for his burning (by one Master Walter Marlar's wife, who was a good nurse unto him, and his very good friend), he made such a prayer of the wedding garment, that some of those that were present were in such great admiration, that their eyes were as thoroughly occupied in looking on him, as their ears gave place to hear his prayer. At his departing out of the chamber, he made likewise a prayer, and gave money to every servant and officer of the house, with exhortation to them to fear and serve God, continually labouring to eschew all manner of evil. That done, he turned him to the wall, and prayed vehemently, that his words might not be spoken in vain, but that the Lord would work the same in them effectually, for his Christ's sake. Then being beneath in the court all the prisoners cried out to him, and bade him farewell, as the rest of the house had done before, with weeping tears.

"The time they carried him to Newgate was about eleven or twelve o'clock in the night, when it was thought none would be stirring abroad; and yet, contrary to their expectation in that behalf, was there in Cheapside, and other places between the Compter and Newgate, a great multitude of people that came to see him, which most gently bade him farewell, praying for him with most lamentable and pitiful tears; and he again as gently bade them farewell, praying most heartily for them and their welfare. Now whether it were a commandment from the Queen and her council, or from Bonner and his adherents, or whether it were merely devised of the Lord Mayor, Aldermen, and Sheriffs of London, or no, I cannot tell; but a great noise there was overnight about the city by divers, that Bradford should be burnt the next day in Smithfield, by four of the clock in the morning, before it should be greatly known to any . . . But . . . the people prevented the device suspected: for the next day,' Monday, July 1, 'at the said hour of four o'clock in the morning, there was in Smithfield such a multitude of men and women, that many being in admiration thereof thought it was not possible that they could have warning of his death, being so great a number in so short a time, unless it were by the singular providence of Almighty God.

"Well, this took not effect as the people thought; for that morning it was nine o'clock of the day before Master Bradford was brought into Smithfield; who, in going through Newgate thitherward, spied a friend of his whom he loved, standing on the one side of the way to the keeper's houseward, unto whom he reached his hand over the people, and plucked him to him, and delivered to him from his head his velvet night-cap, and also his handkerchief, with other things besides. . . . After a little secret talk with him, and each of them parting from other, immediately came to him a brother-in-law of his called Roger Beswick, who as soon as he had taken the said Bradford by the hand, one of the Sheriffs of London, called Woodrofe, came with his staff, and brake the said Roger's head, that the blood ran about his shoulders; which sight Bradford beholding with grief bade his brother farewell, willing him to commend him to his mother and the rest of his friends, and to get him to some surgeon betimes: so they, departing, had little or no talk at all together. Then was he led forth to Smithfield with a great company of weaponed men, to conduct him thither, as the like was not seen at any man's burning: for in every corner of Smithfield there were some, besides those which stood about the stake. Bradford then, being come to the place, fell flat to the ground, secretly making his prayers to Almighty God. And he lying prostrate on the one side of the stake, and a young man, an apprentice, John Leaf, who suffered with him on the other side, they lay flat on their faces, praying to themselves the space of a minute of an hour. Then one of the

Sheriffs said to Master Bradford, 'Arise, and make an end; for the press of the people is great.'

"At that word they both stood up upon their feet; and then Master Bradford took a faggot in his hand, and kissed it, and so likewise the stake. And, when he had so done, he desired of the Sheriffs that his servant might have his raiment; 'for,' said he, 'I have nothing else to give him, and besides that he is a poor man.' And the Sheriff said he should have it. And so forthwith Master Bradford did put off his raiment, and went to the stake; and, holding up his hands, and casting his countenance up to heaven, he said thus, 'O England, England, repent thee of thy sins, repent thee of thy sins. Beware of idolatry, beware of false antichrists: take heed they do not deceive you.' And, as he was speaking these words, the Sheriff bade tie his hands, if he would not be quiet. 'O Master Sheriff,' said Master Bradford, 'I am quiet: God forgive you this, Master Sheriff.' And one of the officers which made the fire, hearing Master Bradford so speaking to the Sheriff, said, 'If you have no better learning than that, you are but a fool, and were best to hold your peace.' To the which words Master Bradford gave no answer, but asked all the world forgiveness, and forgave all the world, and prayed the people to pray for him, and turned his head unto the young man that suffered with him, and said, 'Be of good comfort, brother; for we shall have a merry supper with the Lord this night;' and so spake no more words that any man did hear, but embracing the reeds said thus: "Strait is the way, and narrow is the gate, that leadeth to eternal salvation, and few there be that find it.' "

There seems to have been something peculiarly beautiful and attractive in Bradford's character, exceeding that of other Reformers. "Fuller remarks: 'It is a demonstration to me that he was of a sweet temper, because Parsons, who will hardly afford a good word to a Protestant, saith "that he seemed to be of a more soft and mild nature than many of his fellows." Indeed he was a most holy and mortified man, who secretly in his closet would so weep for his sins, one would have thought he would never have smiled again; and then, appearing in public, he would be so harmlessly pleasant, one would think he had never wept before.'

"The familiar story, that, on seeing evil-doers taken to the place of execution, he was wont to exclaim, 'But for the grace of God there goes John Bradford,' is a universal tradition, which has overcome the lapse of time. And Venning, writing in 1653, desirous to show that, 'by the sight of others' sins, men may learn to bewail their own sinfulness and heart of corruption,' instances the case of Bradford, who, 'when he saw any drunk or heard any swear, &c, would railingly complain, "Lord, I have a drunken head; Lord, I have a swearing heart."

"His personal appearance and daily habits are graphically described by Foxe. 'He was, of person, a tall man, slender, spare of body, somewhat a faint sanguine colour, with an auburn beard. He slept not commonly above four hours a night; and in his bed, till sleep came, his book went not out of his hand. . . . His painful diligence, reading, and prayer, I might almost account it his whole life. He did not eat above one meal a day, which was but very little when he took it; and his continual study was upon his knees. In the midst of dinner he used oftentimes to muse with himself, having his hat over his eyes, from whence came commonly plenty of tears, dropping on his trencher. Very gentle he was to man and child. . . . His chief recreation was in no gaming or other pastime, but only in honest company and comely talk, wherein he would spend a little leisure after dinner at the board, and so to prayer and his book again. He counted that hour not well-spent, wherein he did not some good, either with his pen, study, or exhortation to others."

Mr Townsend concludes his excellent biography with the following passage, which is so true and good that I give it in its entirety. "He may be said to have lived a long life in a short space of time. From his ordination as deacon to the hour of martyrdom he was only permitted to exercise the ministerial office for five years, of which no fewer than two were passed in prison. Until the great day, when the secrets of all hearts shall be revealed, it cannot be fully known to what extent England has been indebted to the labours and the prayers of this devoted man. 'Certainly he was neither the least able nor the least learned' of the fathers of the English Church. He happily combined judgment with 'learning, elocution, sweetness of temper, and profound devotion toward God: . . . and of his worth the Papists themselves were so sensible, that they took more pains to bring him off from the profession of religion than any other.' Had Edward longer occupied the English throne Bradford would have been raised to the episcopal bench. He obtained from the great Bishop of souls a higher promotion. By the holiness of his life and the testimony of his writings 'he yet speaketh.' By the flames of martyrdom 'Bradford and Latimer, Cranmer and Ridley, four prime pillars of the Reformed Church of England,' have, through the grace of God, lighted such a candle in this country as shall never be extinguished."

Bradford's literary remains occupy about 1100 pages, and fill two volumes of the Parker Society's series. They consist chiefly of sermons, short treatises, meditations, prayers, declarations, exhortations, and letters. All are good, and all deserve reading. If I must pick out any of his writings as specially good, I would name his controversial treatises, entitled, "A Confutation of four Romish Doctrines," and "The Hurt of Hearing Mass;" his sermons on Repentance and the Lord's Supper; his Treatise against the fear of death; and his Farewells to London, Cambridge, Lancashire, Cheshire, etc. Above all, I commend his 100 letters to friends. He that can read any of the above-mentioned writings without feeling his soul stirred within him, must be in an unsatisfactory condition. To my mind, there is not only Scriptural soundness in all that Bradford writes, but a peculiar fire, unction, warmth, and directness, which entitle him to a very high rank among Christian authors. Had he lived longer and written more, one fancies it would have been an immense blessing to the Church.

My first extract shall be taken from Bradford's "Treatise against the Fear of Death." (Vol. i., page 342, Parker Society's edition.)

"Some man will say, O Sir, if I were certain that I should depart from this miserable life into that so great felicity, then could I be right glad, and rejoice as you will me, and bid death welcome. But I am a sinner; I have grievously transgressed and broken God's will; and therefore I am afraid I shall be sent into eternal woe, perdition, and misery.

"Here, my brother, thou doest well that thou dost acknowledge thyself a sinner, and to have deserved eternal death; for, doubtless, 'if we say we have no sin, we are liars, and the truth is not in us.' A child of a night's birth is not pure in God's sight. In sin were we born, and 'by birth (or nature) we are the children of wrath' and firebrands of hell: therefore, confess ourselves to be sinners we needs must; for 'if the Lord will observe any man's iniquities, none shall be able to abide it;' yea, we must needs all cry, 'Enter not into judgment, O Lord; for in Thy sight no flesh nor man living can be saved.' In this point, therefore, thou hast done well to confess thyself a sinner.

"But now where thou standest in doubt of pardon of thy sins, and thereby art afraid of damnation, my dear brother, I would have thee answer me one question, that is, 'Whether thou desirest pardon or no; whether thou dost repent nor no; whether thou dost unfeignedly purpose, if thou shouldest live, to amend thy life or no?' If thou dost, even before God, so purpose, and desirest His mercy, then hearken, my good brother, what the Lord saith unto thee:

"I am He, I am He, that for mine own sake will do away thine offences.' 'If thy sins be red as scarlet, they shall be made as white as snow,' for 'I have no pleasure in the death of a sinner.' 'As surely as I live, I will not thy death; but rather that thou shouldest live and be converted.' I 'have so loved the world,' that I would not spare my dearly beloved Son, the image of my substance and brightness of my glory, 'by whom all things are made,' by whom all things were given; but gave Him for thee, not only to be man, but also to take thy nature, and to purge it from mortality, sin, and all corruption, and to adorn and endue it with immortality and eternal glory, not only in His own person, but also in thee and for thee: whereof now by faith I would have thee certain, as in very deed thou shalt at length feel and fully enjoy for ever. This my Son I have given to the death, and that a most shameful death, 'even of the cross,' for thee 'to destroy death,' to satisfy my justice for thy sins; therefore 'believe,' and 'according to thy faith, so be it unto thee.'

"Hearken what my Son Himself saith to thee: 'Come unto Me all ye that labour, and are heavy laden, and I will refresh you;' 'I came not into the world to damn the world, but to save it.' 'I came not to call the righteous, but sinners to repentance.' I pray not,' saith He, 'for these mine Apostles only, but also for all them that by their preaching shall believe in Me.' Now what prayed He for such? 'Father,' saith He, 'I will that where I am they may also be, that they may see and enjoy the glory I have, and always had with Thee. Father, save them and keep them in Thy truth,'

'Father,' saith He, 'I sanctify myself, and offer up myself for them.' Lo, thus thou hearest how My Son prayeth for thee.

"Mark now what my Apostle Paul saith: 'We know,' saith he, 'that our Saviour Christ's prayers were heard;' also, 'This is a true saying, that Jesus Christ came into the world to save sinners.' Hearken what he saith to the jailer, 'Believe in the Lord Jesus Christ, and thou shalt be saved;' for He, by His own self, hath 'made purgation for our sins.' 'To Him,' saith Peter, 'bear all the prophets witness, that whosoever believeth in His name shall receive remission of their sins.' 'Believe,' man. Pray, 'Lord, help mine unbelief;' 'Lord, increase my faith.' 'Ask, and thou shalt have.' Hearken what St John saith: 'If we confess our sins, God is righteous to forgive us all our iniquities; and the blood of our Lord Jesus Christ shall cleanse us from all our sins;' for, 'if we sin, we have an Advocate,' saith he, 'with the Father, Jesus Christ the righteous, and He is the propitiation for our sins.' Hearken what Christ is called: 'Call His name Jesus,' saith the angel; 'for He shall save His people from their sins:' so that 'where abundance of sin is, there is abundance of grace.'

"Say, therefore, 'Who shall lay anything to my charge? It is God that absolveth me, Who then shall condemn me? It is Christ which is dead for my sins, yea, which is risen for my righteousness, and sitteth on the right hand of the Father, and prayeth for me.' Be certain, therefore, and sure of pardon of thy sins; be certain and sure of everlasting life. Do not say in thy heart, 'Who shall descend into the deep?' that is, doubt not of pardon of thy sins, for that is to fetch up Christ. Neither say thou, 'Who shall ascend up into heaven?' that is, doubt not of eternal bliss, for that is to put Christ out of heaven. But mark what the Lord saith unto thee, 'The Word is nigh thee, even in thy mouth and in thy heart; and this is the word of faith which we preach: If thou confess with thy mouth that Jesus Christ is the Lord, and believe with thy heart that God raised Him up from the dead, thou shalt be safe.' If thou 'believe that Jesus Christ died and rose again,' even so shalt thou be assured, saith the Lord God, that 'dying with Christ, I will bring thee again with Him.'

"Thus, dear brother, I thought good to write to thee, in the name of the Lord, that thou, fearing death for nothing else but because of thy sins, mightest be assured of pardon of them; and so embrace death as a dear friend, and insult against his terror, sting, and power; saying, 'Death, where is thy sting? Hell, where is thy victory?' Nothing in all the world so displeaseth the Lord as to doubt of His mercy. In the mouth of two or three witnesses we should be content; therefore, in that thou hast heard so many witnesses, how that indeed desiring mercy with the Lord, thou art not sent empty away, give credit thereto, and say with the good Virgin Mary, 'Behold Thy servant, O Lord; be it unto me according to Thy word.' "

My second extract shall be taken from Bradford's "Farewell to Lancashire and Cheshire." (Vol. i., p. 449.)

"When I consider the cause of my condemnation, I cannot but lament that I do no more rejoice than I do, for it is God's verity and truth. The condemnation is not a condemnation of Bradford simply, but rather a condemnation of Christ and His truth. Bradford is nothing else but an instrument, in whom Christ and His doctrine are condemned; and, therefore, my dearly beloved, rejoice, rejoice, and give thanks with me, and for me, that ever God did vouchsafe so great a benefit to our country, as to choose the most unworthy (I mean myself) to be one in whom it would please Him to suffer any kind of affliction, much more this violent kind of death, which I perceive is prepared for me with you for His sake. All glory and praise be given unto God our Father for this His exceeding great mercy towards me, through Jesus Christ our Lord. Amen.

"But perchance you will say unto me, 'What is the cause for which you are condemned? We hear say that ye deny all presence of Christ in His holy Supper, and so make it a bare sign and common bread, and nothing else.' My dearly beloved, what is said of me, and will be, I cannot tell. It is told me that Master Pendleton is gone down to preach to you, not as he once recanted (for you all know how he hath preached contrary to that he was wont to preach afore I came amongst you), but to recant that which he had recanted. How he will speak of me, and report before I come, when I am come, and when I am burned, I much pass not; for he that is so uncertain, and will speak so often against himself, I cannot think he will speak well of me, except it make for his purpose and profit; but of this enough.

"Indeed, the chief thing I am condemned for as an heretic is, because I deny the sacrament of the altar, which is not Christ's Supper, but a plain perverting of it (being used, as the Papists now use it, to be a real, natural, and corporal presence of Christ's body and blood, under the forms and accidents of bread and wine): that is, because I deny transubstantiation, which is the darling of the devil, and daughter and heir to Antichrist's religion, whereby the Mass is maintained, Christ's Supper perverted, the ministry taken away, repentance repelled, and all true godliness abandoned.

"In the Supper of our Lord, or sacrament of Christ's body and blood, I confess and believe that there is a true and very presence of whole Christ, God and Man, to the faith of the receiver (but not of the stander by or looker on), as there is a very true presence of bread and wine to the senses of him that is partaker thereof. This faith, this doctrine, which consenteth with the Word of God, and with the true testimony of Christ's Church, which the Popish Church doth persecute, will I not forsake; and therefore am I condemned as an heretic, and shall be burned.

"But, my dearly beloved, this truth (which I have taught and you have received, I believed and do believe, and therein give my life), I hope in God shall never be burned, bound, nor overcome, but shall triumph, have victory, and be at liberty, maugre the head of all God's adversaries. For there is no counsel against the Lord, nor no device of man can be able to defeat the verity in any other than in such as be 'children of unbelief,' which have no 'love to the truth,' and, therefore, are given up to believe lies. From which plague the Lord of mercies deliver you and all this realm, my dear hearts in the Lord, I humbly beseech His mercy. Amen."

My third and last extract shall be taken from a letter written by Bradford to Francis Russell, Earl of Bedford, in the year 1554. (Bradford's Works, Vol. ii., p. 79.)

"You have cause, my good lord, to be thankful. For look upon your vocation, I pray you, and tell me how many noblemen, earls' sons, lords, knights, and men of estimation hath God in this realm of England dealt thus withal. I daresay you think not you have deserved this. Only God's mercy in Christ hath wrought this on you, as He did in Jeremy's time on Ebedmelech, in Ahab's time on Obadiah, in Christ's time on Joseph of Arimathaea, in the

Apostles' time on Sergius Paulus and the Queen Candace's chamberlain. Only now be thankful, and continue, continue, continue, my good lord, continue to confess Christ. Be not ashamed of Him before men, for then will not He be ashamed of you. Now will He try you: stick fast unto Him, and He will stick fast by you; He will be with you in trouble and deliver you. But then you must cry unto Him, for so it proceedeth: 'He cried unto Me, and I heard: I was with him in trouble.'

"Remember Lot's wife, which looked back; remember Francis Spira; remember that 'none is crowned, except he strive lawfully.' Remember that all you have is at Christ's commandment. Remember He lost more for you than you can lose for Him. Remember you lose not that which is lost for His sake, for you shall find much more here and elsewhere. Remember you shall die; and when and where and how you cannot tell. Remember the death of sinners is most terrible. Remember the death of God's saints is precious in His sight. Remember the multitude goeth the wide way which windeth to woe. Remember the strait gate which leadeth to glory hath but few travellers. Remember Christ biddeth you strive to enter in thereat. Remember he that trusteth in the Lord shall receive strength to stand against all the assaults of his enemies.

"Be certain all the hairs of your head are numbered. Be certain your good Father hath appointed bounds, over the which the devil dare not look. Commit yourself to Him; He is, hath been, and will be your Keeper; cast your care on Him, and He will care for you. Let Christ be your scope and mark to prick at; let Him be your pattern to work by; let Him be your example to follow: give Him as your heart so your hand, as your mind so your tongue, as your faith so your feet; and let His Word be your candle to be before you in all matters of religion.

"Blessed is he that walketh not to these Popish prayers, nor standeth at them, nor sitteth at them. Glorify God both in soul and body. He that gathereth not with Christ scattereth abroad. Use prayer; look for God's help, which is at hand to them that ask and hope thereafter assuredly. In which prayer I heartily desire your lordship to remember us, who as we are going with you right gladly, God be praised, so we look to go before you, hoping that you will follow if God so will."

Comment upon these extracts, I think my readers will agree, is needless. They speak for themselves. Scores of similar passages might easily be selected, if space permitted. But enough is as good as a feast. Enough, perhaps, has been quoted to prove that Bradford's literary remains are well worth reading.

Let us thank God that the foundations of the Reformed Church of England were laid by such men as John Bradford. Let us clearly understand what kind of men our martyred Reformers were, what kind of doctrines they held, and what kind of lives they lived. Let us pray that the work they did for the Church of England may never be despised or underrated. Above all, let us pray that there never may be wanting among us a continual succession of English clergy, who shall keep the martyrs' candle burning brightly, and shall hand down true Reformation principles to our children's children.

NICHOLAS RIDLEY: BISHOP AND MARTYR

Nicholas Ridley, Bishop and Martyr, is a man whose name ought to be a household word among all true-hearted English Churchmen. In the noble army of English Reformers, no one deserves a higher place than Ridley. Together with Cranmer, Latimer, and Hooper, he occupies the first rank among the worthies of our blessed Reformation, and in point of real merit is second to none. Ridley was born about the year 1503, at Willymotiswick, in Northumberland, not far from the Scottish border. His early education was received at a school at Newcastle-on-Tyne, and in the year 1518 he was removed to Pembroke College, Cambridge. Here he soon became distinguished as a student of uncommon diligence and ability, and rapidly rose to a prominent position in the University. He became Fellow of Pembroke in 1524, Chaplain to the University in 1532, Senior Proctor in 1533, and Master of Pembroke in 1540.

The beginnings of Ridley's decided Protestantism are wrapped in some obscurity. Like Cranmer, he seems to have worked his way gradually into the full light of Scriptural truth, and not to have attained full maturity of soundness in faith at once. He signed the decree against the Pope's supremacy in 1534. In 1537 he became Chaplain to Archbishop Cranmer, and was appointed by him to the Vicarage of Herne, in East Kent, in 1538. Here, in the retirement of a quiet country parsonage, he first read the famous treatise of Ratramnus, or Bertram, about the Lord's Supper, and was led by it to search the Scriptures, and examine more carefully than before the writings of the Fathers. The result was, that he began to entertain grave doubts of the truth of the Romish doctrine about the Lord's Supper. These doubts he communicated to his friend and patron the Archbishop. The final event was the conviction of both Cranmer and Ridley that the received tenet of transubstantiation was unscriptural, novel, and erroneous. It was not, however, till the year 1545 that Ridley completely renounced the doctrine of the corporal presence of Christ's body and blood in the Sacrament. About that time, the arguments and sufferings of Frith, Lambert, and others, confirmed the impressions received at Herne, and he unhesitatingly embraced the doctrine of the Lord's Supper as now held in the Church of England, and never swerved from it till his death.

In 1540 Ridley became Chaplain to Henry VIII, and then rose from office to office of dignity and influence with rapid steps. In 1541 he was made Prebendary of Canterbury, and in 1545 a Prebendary of Westminster. In 1547 he was appointed Vicar of Soham, and in the same year was nominated Bishop of Rochester by Henry VIII. In 1550 he was made Bishop of London by Edward VI, and in 1553 was nominated Bishop of Durham. This last change of position, however, never took place. The lamented death of the young King Edward put a complete stop to Ridley's earthly honours. In 1553 he was excepted by name from the amnesty by Bloody Queen Mary, who had special dislike to him, and was committed to the Tower.

The circumstances under which Ridley came into direct collision with Queen Mary before the death of Edward VI are so graphically described by Foxe that I think it best to give them in the Martyrologist's own words:

"About the eighth of September, 1552, Dr Ridley, then Bishop of London, lying at his house at Hadham in Herts, went to visit the Lady Mary, then lying at Hunsden, two miles off, and was gently entertained of Sir Thomas Wharton and other her officers, till it was almost eleven of the clock, about which time the said Lady Mary came forth into her chamber of presence, and then the said Bishop there saluted her Grace, and said that he was come to do this duty to her Grace. Then she thanked him for his pains, and for a quarter of an hour talked with him very pleasantly, and said that she knew him in the court when he was chaplain to her father, and could well remember a sermon that he made before King Henry her father at the marriage of my Lady Clinton that now is, to Sir Anthony Brown, &c., and so dismissed him to dine with her officers. After the dinner was done, the Bishop being called for by the said Lady Mary, resorted again to her Grace, between whom this communication was. First the Bishop beginneth in manner as followeth. 'Madam, I came not only to do my duty to see your Grace, but also to offer myself to preach before you on Sunday next, if it will please you to hear me.'

"At this her countenance changed, and after silence for a space, she answered thus: 'My Lord, as for this last matter, I pray you make the answer to it yourself.'

"*Ridley.* 'Madam, considering mine office and calling, I am bound in duty to make your Grace this offer to preach before you.'

"*Mary.* 'Well, I pray you, make the answer, as I have said, to this matter yourself, for you know the answer well enough; but if there be no remedy, but I must make you answer, this shall be your answer: the door of the parish church adjoining shall be open for you, if you come, and ye may preach if you list, but neither I nor any of mine shall hear you.'

"*Ridley.* 'Madam, I trust you will not refuse God's Word.'

"*Mary.* 'I cannot tell what ye call God's Word—that is not God's Word now, that was God's Word in my father's days.'

"*Ridley.* 'God's Word is all one in all times, but hath been better understood and practised in some ages than in other.'

"*Mary.* 'You durst not for your ears have avouched that for God's Word in my father's days that now you do; and as for your new books, I thank God I never read any of them, I never did nor ever will do.'

"And after many bitter words against the form of religion then established, and against the government of the realm, and the laws made in the young years of her brother, which she said she was not bound to obey till her brother came to perfect age, and then she said she would obey them, she asked the Bishop whether he were one of the council? He answered, 'No.' 'You might well enough,' said she, 'as the council goeth nowadays.' And so she concluded with these words: 'My Lord, for your gentleness to come and see me I thank you, but for your offering to preach before me I thank you never a whit.'

"Then the said Bishop was brought by Sir Thomas Wharton to the place where they had dined, and was desired to drink, and after he had drunk, he paused awhile, looking very sadly, and suddenly brake out into these words, 'Surely I have done amiss.' 'Why so?' quoth Sir Thomas Wharton. 'For I have drunk, said he, 'in that place where God's Word offered hath been refused, whereas if I had remembered my duty, I ought to have departed immediately, and to have shaken off the dust of my shoes for a testimony against this house.' These words were by the said Bishop spoken with such a vehemency, that some of the hearers afterward confessed their hair to stand upright on their heads. This done, the said Bishop departed, and so returned to his house."

From the Tower Ridley was sent to Oxford in 1554, to be baited and insulted in a mock disputation; and finally, after two years' imprisonment, was burned at Oxford with old Latimer, on October 16th, 1555. Singularly enough, he seems to have had forebodings of the kind of death he would die. Humphrey, in his "Life of Jewel," records the following anecdote: "Ridley, on one occasion, being tossed about in a great storm, exhorted his terrified companions with these words, 'Be of good cheer, and bend to your oars; this boat carries a Bishop who is not to be drowned, but burned.' "

From the day that Ridley became a Bishop, he appears to have been wholly absorbed in assisting Archbishop Cranmer to establish and consolidate the Reformation of the Church of England. For this huge and formidable work he was peculiarly well fitted by his acknowledged learning. To no one, perhaps, of the Reformers are we more indebted for our admirable Articles and Liturgy, than to Ridley. Altered and somewhat improved, as they undoubtedly were in Queen Elizabeth's time, we must never forget that in their rudimentary form they first received shape and consistency from the Edwardian Reformers; and that, of the Edwardian Reformers, no one probably did a greater portion of the work than Bishop Ridley. In fact, the importance of his work in the English Reformation may be gathered from the saying of one of his most distinguished adversaries: "Latimer leaneth to Cranmer, Cranmer leaneth to Ridley, and Ridley leaneth to his own singular wit." No one, certainly, seems to have had more influence over the mind of Edward VI than Ridley. It was owing to his suggestion that the noble-minded young King founded no less than sixteen grammar schools, including Christ's Hospital; and designed, if his life had been spared, to erect twelve colleges for the education of youth. Besides this, the noble institution of St Bartholomew's Hospital, in Smithfield, was first endowed and called into existence by Ridley's advice to the King.[1]

The account given by Mr Christmas, in his biography prefixed to Ridley's works, of the circumstances under which Edward VI founded St Bartholomew's Hospital is so interesting that I shall give it in its entirety:

"A remarkable instance of the beneficial effect of Ridley's counsels is to be seen in the foundation of three institutions in the reign of Edward VI, and which in point of date may be called the first fruits of the Reformation. Both in the council chamber and the pulpit did this eminent prelate resist the sacrilegious spirit of his day; and though the young King was but partially able to resist the tide of corruption, he yet founded, at the suggestion of Ridley, no less than sixteen grammar schools, and designed, had his life been spared, to erect twelve colleges for the education of youth. Shortly before his death he sent for the Bishop, and thanking him for a sermon in which he strongly pressed the duty of providing for the poverty and ignorance of our fellow-men, added: 'I took myself to be especially touched by your speech, as well in regard of the abilities God hath given me, as in regard of the example which from me He will require; for as in the kingdom I am next under God, so must I most nearly approach Him in goodness and mercy; for as our miseries stand most in need of aid from Him, so are we the greatest debtors—debtors to all that are miserable, and shall be the greatest accountants of our dispensa tion therein; and therefore, my Lord, as you have given me, I thank you, this general exhortation, so direct me (I pray you) by what particular actions I may this way best discharge my duty.' The Bishop, who was not prepared for such a request, begged time to consider, and to consult with those who were more conversant with the condition of the poor. Having taken the advice of the Lord Mayor and Aldermen of London, he shortly returned to the King, representing that there appeared to be three different classes of poor. Some were poor by impotency of nature, as young fatherless children, old decrepit persons, idiots, cripples, and such like; these required to be educated and maintained; for

[1] Actually the hospital was originally founded in 1123.

them accordingly the King gave up the Grey Friars' Church, near Newgate Market, now called Christ's Hospital. Others he observed were poor by faculty, as wounded soldiers, diseased and sick persons who required to be cured and relieved; for their use the King gave St Bartholomew's, near Smithfield; the third sort were poor by idleness or unthriftiness, as vagabonds, loiterers, &c., who should be chastised and reduced to good order; for these the King appointed his house at Bridewell, the ancient mansion of many English Kings."

The inner life and habits of Ridley, during the brief period of his episcopate, are so beautifully described by Foxe in his "Acts and Monuments" that I make no excuse for giving the passage in its entirety:

"In his calling and offices he so travelled and occupied himself by preaching and teaching the true and wholesome doctrine of Christ, that never good child was more singularly loved of his dear parents than he of his flock and diocese. Every holiday and Sunday he lightly preached in some one place or other, except he were otherwise letted by weighty affairs and business. To whose sermons the people resorted, swarming about him like bees, and coveting the sweet flowers and wholesome juice of the fruitful doctrine, which he did not only preach, but showed the same by his life, as a glittering lantern to the eyes and senses of the blind, in such pure order and chastity of life (declining from evil desires and concupiscences), that even his very enemies could not reprove him in any one iota thereof.

"Besides this, he was passingly well learned. His memory was great, and he of such reading withal, that of right he deserved to be comparable to the best of this our age, as can testify as well divers his notable works, pithy sermons, and sundry disputations in both the Universities, as also his very adversaries, all which will say no less themselves.

"Besides all this, he was wise of counsel, deep of wit, and very politic in all his doings. How merciful and careful he was to reduce the obstinate Papists from their erroneous opinions, and by gentleness to win them to the truth, his gentle ordering and courteous handling of Doctor Heath, late Archbishop of York, being prisoner with him in King Edward's time in his house one year, sufficiently declareth. In fine, he was such a prelate, and in all points so good, godly, and spiritual a man, that England may justly rue the loss of so worthy a treasure. And thus hitherto concerning these public matters.

"Now will I speak something further particularly of his person and conditions. He was a man right comely and well proportioned in all points, both in complexion and lineaments of the body. He took all things in good part, bearing no malice nor rancour from his heart, but straightways forgetting all injuries and offences done against him. He was very kind and natural to his kinsfolk, and yet not bearing with them anything otherwise than right would require, giving them always for a general rule (yea, to his own brother and sister) that they doing evil should seek or look for nothing at his hand, but should be as strangers and aliens unto him, and they to be his brother or sister which used honesty and a godly trade of life.

"He, using all kinds of ways to mortify himself, was given to much prayer and contemplation; for duly every morning, so soon as his apparel was done upon him, he went forthwith to his bedchamber, and there upon his knees prayed the space of half-an-hour, which being done, immediately he went to his study (if there came no other business to interrupt him), where he continued till ten of the clock, and then came to common prayer, daily used in his house. The prayers being done he went to dinner, where he used little talk, except otherwise occasion by some had been ministered, and then it was sober, discreet, and wise, and sometimes merry, as cause required.

"The dinner done, which was not very long, he used to sit an hour or thereabouts talking or playing at chess. That done, he returned to his study, and there would continue, except suitors or business abroad were occasion of the contrary, until five of the clock at night, and then would come to common prayer, as in the forenoon, which being finished he went to supper, behaving himself there as at his dinner before. After supper recreating himself in playing at chess the space of an hour, he would then return again to his study; continuing there till eleven of the clock at night, which was his common hour to go to bed, then saying his prayers upon his knees, as in the morning when he rose. Being at his manor of Fulham, as divers times he used to be, he read daily a lecture to his family at the common prayer, beginning at the Acts of the Apostles, and so going throughout all the Epistles of St Paul, giving to every man that could read a New Testament, hiring them besides with money to learn by heart certain principal chapters, but especially the thirteenth chapter of the Acts; reading also unto his household oftentimes the one hundred and first Psalm, being marvellous careful over his family, that they might be a spectacle of all virtue and honesty to other. To be short, as he was as godly and virtuous himself, so nothing but virtue and godliness reigned in his house, feeding them with the food of our Saviour Jesus Christ."

"Now remaineth a word or two to be declared of his gentle nature and kindly pity in the usage of an old woman called Mistress Bonner, mother to Doctor Bonner, sometime Bishop of London: which I thought good to touch, as well for the rare clemency of Doctor Ridley, as the unworthy immanity[1] and ungrateful disposition again of Doctor Bonner. Bishop Ridley, being at his manor of Fulham, always sent for the said Mistress Bonner, dwelling in an house adjoining to his house, to dinner and supper, with one Mistress Mungey, Bonner's sister, saying, 'Go for my mother Bonner,' who coming, was ever placed in the chair at the table's end, being so gently entreated, welcomed, and taken, as though he had been born of her own body, being never displaced of her seat, although the King's council had been present, saying, when any of them were there (as divers times they were), 'By your lordships' favour, this place of right and custom is for my mother Bonner.' But how well he was recompensed for this his singular gentleness and pitiful pity after at the hands of the said Doctor Bonner, almost the least child that goeth by the ground can declare. For who afterward was more enemy to Ridley than Bonner and his? Who more went about to seek his destruction than he, recompensing his gentleness with extreme cruelty? As well appeared by the strait handling of Ridley's own natural sister, and George Shipside, her husband, from time to time. The gentleness of Ridley did suffer Bonner's mother, sister, and other his kindred, not only quietly to enjoy all that which they had of Bonner, but also entertained them in his house, showing much courtesy and friendship daily unto them. On the

[1] immanity = inhuman cruelty

other side Bishop Bonner, being restored again, would not suffer the brother and natural sister of Bishop Ridley, and other his friends, not only to enjoy that which they had by the said their brother Bishop Ridley, but also currishly, without all order of law or honesty, by extort power wrested from them all the livings they had.

"And yet being not therewith satisfied, he sought all the means he could to work the death of the aforesaid Shipside, saying that he would make twelve godfathers to go upon him; which had been brought to pass indeed, at what time he was prisoner at Oxford, had not God otherwise wrought his deliverance by means of Doctor Heath, Bishop then of Worcester.

"Whereby all good indifferent readers notoriously have to understand, what great diversity was in the disposition of these two natures. Whereof as the one excelled in mercy and pity, so the other again as much or more excelled in churlish ingratitude and despiteful disdain. But of this matter enough."

The closing scene of Ridley's life, his famous martyrdom, on October 16th, 1555, is described with such touching and masterly simplicity by Foxe, that I think it best to let my readers have it in the Martyrologist's own words:

"Upon the north side of the town of Oxford, in the ditch over against Balliol College, the place of execution was appointed; and for fear of any tumult that might arise, to let the burning of them, the Lord Williams was commanded, by the Queen's letters, and the householders of the city to be there assistant, sufficiently appointed. And when everything was in a readiness, the prisoners were brought forth by the mayor and the bailiffs.

"Master Ridley had a fair black gown furred, and faced with foins, such as he was wont to wear, being Bishop, and tippet of velvet furred likewise about his neck, a velvet nightcap upon his head, and a corner cap upon the same, going in a pair of slippers to the stake, and going between the mayor and an alderman.

"After him came Master Latimer, in a poor Bristol frieze frock, all worn, with his buttoned cap, and a kerchief on his head, all ready to the fire, a new long shroud hanging over his hose down to the feet. All this at the first sight stirred men's hearts to rue upon them, beholding on the one side the honour they sometime had, and on the other the calamity whereunto they were fallen.

"Then Master Ridley, looking back, espied Master Latimer coming after, unto whom he said, 'Oh, be ye there?' 'Yea,' said Master Latimer, 'Have after you as fast as I can follow.' So he following a pretty way off. At length they came both to the stake, the one after the other; where first Dr Ridley entering the place, and marvellous earnestly holding up both his hands, looked towards heaven. Then shortly after espying Master Latimer, with a wondrous cheerful look he ran to him, embraced and kissed him; and, as they that stood near reported, comforted him, saying, 'Be of good heart, brother, for God will either assuage the fury of the flame, or else strengthen us to abide it.'

"With that went he to the stake, kneeled down by it, kissed it and effectually prayed; and behind him Master Latimer kneeled, as earnestly calling upon God as he. After they arose the one talked with the other a little while, while they which were appointed to see the execution removed themselves out of the sun. What they said I can learn of no man.

After a sermon by a renegade preacher named Smith, which they were not allowed to answer, "they were commanded to make them ready, which they with all meekness obeyed. Master Ridley took his gown and his tippet, and gave it to his brother-in-law Master Shipside, who all his time of imprisonment, although he might not be suffered to come to him, lay there at his own charges to provide him necessaries, which, from time to time, he sent him by the sergeant that kept him. Some other of his apparel that was little worth he gave away; other the bailiffs took.

"He gave away besides divers other small things to gentlemen standing by, and divers of them pitifully weeping. As to Sir Henry Lea, he gave a new groat; and to divers of my lord Williams' gentlemen some napkins, some nutmegs, and rases of ginger; his dial, and such other things as he had about him, to every one that stood next him. Some plucked the points off his hose. Happy was he that might get any rag of him.

"Master Latimer gave nothing, but quietly suffered his keeper to pull off his hose and his other array, which to look unto was very simple; and being stripped unto his shroud, he seemed as comely a person to them that were there present, as one should lightly see; and whereas in his clothes he appeared a withered and crooked silly old man, he now stood bolt upright, as comely a father as one might lightly behold.

"Then Master Ridley, standing as yet in his truss, said to his brother, 'It were best for me to go in my truss still.' 'No,' quoth his brother, 'it will put you to more pain; and the truss will do a poor man good.' Whereunto Master Ridley said, 'Be it so, in the name of God;' and so unlaced himself. Then, being in his shirt, he stood upon the aforesaid stone, and held up his hand and said, 'O heavenly Father, I give unto Thee most hearty thanks, for that Thou hast called me to be a professor of Thee, even unto death. I beseech Thee, Lord God, take mercy upon this realm of England, and deliver the same from all her enemies.'

"Then the smith took a chain of iron, and brought the same about both Dr Ridley's and Master Latimer's middles: and as he was knocking in a staple, Dr Ridley took the chain in his hand, and shaked the same, for it did gird in his belly, and looking aside to the smith said, 'Good fellow, knock it in hard, for the flesh will have his course.' Then his brother did bring him gunpowder in a bag, and would have tied the same about his neck. Master Ridley asked what it was. His brother said, 'Gunpowder.' 'Then,' said he, 'I will take it to be sent of God; therefore I will receive it as sent of Him. And have you any,' said he, 'for my brother?' meaning Master Latimer. 'Yea, sir, that I have,' quoth his brother. 'Then give it unto him,' said he, 'betime; lest ye come too late.' So his brother went, and carried of the same gunpowder unto Master Latimer.

"Then they brought a faggot, kindled with fire, and laid the same down at Dr Ridley's feet. To whom Master Latimer spake in this manner: 'BE OF GOOD COMFORT, MASTER RIDLEY, AND PLAY THE MAN. WE SHALL THIS DAY LIGHT SUCH A CANDLE, BY GOD'S GRACE, IN ENGLAND, AS I TRUST SHALL NEVER BE PUT OUT.'

"And so the fire being given unto them, when Dr Ridley saw the fire flaming up towards him, he cried with a wonderful loud voice, '*In manus tuas, Domine, commendo spiritum meum: Domine, recipe spiritum meum.*' And after, repeated this latter part often in English, 'Lord, Lord, receive my spirit;' Master Latimer crying as vehemently on the other side, 'O Father of heaven, receive my soul!' who received the flame, as it were embracing of it.

"After that he had stroked his face with his hand, and as it were bathed them a little in the fire, he soon died (as it appeared), with very little pain or none. And thus much concerning the end of this old and blessed servant of God, Master Latimer, for whose laborious travails, fruitful life, and constant death, the whole realm hath cause to give great thanks to Almighty God.

"But Master Ridley, by reason of the evil making of the fire unto him, because the wooden faggots were laid about the gorse, and overhigh built, the fire burned first beneath, being kept down by the wood; which when he felt, he desired them for Christ's sake to let the fire come unto him. Which when his brother-in-law heard, but not well understood, intending to rid him out of his pain (for the which cause he gave attendance), as one in such sorrow not well advised what he did, he heaped faggots upon him, so that he clean covered him, which made the fire more vehement beneath, that it burned clean all his nether parts before it touched the upper; and that made him leap up and down under the faggots, and often desire them to let the fire come unto him, saying, 'I cannot burn.' Which indeed appeared well; for after his legs were consumed, by reason of his struggling through the pain (whereof he had no release but only his contentation in God) he shewed that side towards us clean, shirt and all untouched with flame. Yet in all this torment he forgot not to call unto God still, having in his mouth, 'Lord, have mercy upon me,' intermingling his cry, 'Let the fire come unto me, I cannot burn.' In which pangs he laboured till one of the standers by with his bill pulled off the faggots above, and where he saw the fire flame up, he wrested himself unto that side. And when the flame touched the gunpowder, he was seen to stir no more, but burned on the other side, falling down at Master Latimer's feet; which, some said, happened by reason that the chain loosed; others said, that he fell over the chain by reason of the poise of his body, and the weakness of the nether limbs.

"Some said, that before he was like to fall from the stake, he desired them to hold him to it with their bills. However it was, surely it moved hundreds to tears, in beholding the horrible sight; for I think there was none, that had not clean exiled all humanity and mercy, which would not have lamented to behold the fury of the fire so to rage upon their bodies. Signs there were of sorrow on every side. Some took it grievously to see their deaths, whose lives they held full dear; some pitied their persons, that thought their souls had no need thereof. His brother moved many men, seeing his miserable case, seeing (I say) him compelled to such infelicity, that he thought then to do him best service when he hastened his end. Some cried out of the fortune, to see his endeavour (who most dearly loved him, and sought his release) turn to his greater vexation and increase of pain. But whoso considered their preferments in time past, the places of honour that they some time occupied in this Commonwealth, the favour they were in with their princes, and the opinion of learning they had in the University where they studied, could not choose but sorrow with tears, to see so great dignity, honour, and estimation, so necessary members some time accounted, so many godly virtues, the study of so many years, such excellent learning, to be put into the fire, and consumed in one moment. Well: dead they are and the reward of this world they have already. What reward remaineth for them in heaven, the day of the Lord's glory, when He cometh with His saints, shall shortly, I trust, declare."

It only remains now to give some account of Ridley's writings. They are few in number, and occupy only one volume of the Parker Society's series. They consist chiefly of short treatises against transubstantiation and image-worship; conferences with Latimer and Bourne; a disputation held in 1549, about the sacrament; disputations and examination at Oxford, held shortly before his martyrdom; injunctions to the diocese of London; and thirty-four letters, chiefly written during his imprisonments. Scanty as these literary remains are from so great a divine, they are worthy of his pen, and make us wish he had written more. But, doubtless, the worthy Bishop had little time for writing. To work, and preach, and advise, and witness, and suffer, and die for God's truth, was his appointed lot. And who shall dare to say that his short life and glorious death have not done more for Christ's truth in England than fifty folio volumes of writings?

I venture to think that the following extracts from Ridley's writings will be found interesting.

(1) My first extract shall be taken from Ridley's Conference with Latimer (Parker Society's edition, p. 145):

"In Tynedale, where I was born, not far from the Scottish

borders, I have known my countrymen watch night and day in their harness, such as they had, that is, in their jacks, and their spears in their hands (you call them northern gads), especially when they had any privy warning of the coming of the Scots. And so doing, although at every such bickering some of them spent their lives, yet by such means, like pretty men, they defended their country. And those that so died, I think, that before God, they died in a good quarrel, and their offspring and progeny all the country loved them the better for their fathers' sake.

"And in the quarrel of Christ our Saviour, in the defence of His own Divine ordinances, by which He giveth unto us life and immortality, yea, in the quarrel of faith and Christian religion, wherein resteth our everlasting salvation, shall we not watch? Shall we not go always armed, ever looking when our adversary (which, like a roaring lion, seeketh whom he may devour) shall come upon us by reason of our slothfulness? Yea, and woe be unto us, if he can oppress us at unawares, which undoubtedly he will do, if he find us sleeping. Let us awake therefore; for if the good man of the house knew what hour the thief would come, he would surely watch and not suffer his house to be broken up. Let us awake therefore, I say, and let us not suffer our house to be broken up. 'Resist the devil,' says St James, 'and he will fly from you.' Let us therefore resist him manfully, and, taking the cross upon our shoulders, let us follow our Captain Christ, who by His own blood hath dedicated and hallowed the way, which leadeth unto the Father, that is, to the light which no man can attain, the fountain of everlasting joys. Let us follow, I say, whither He calleth and allureth us, that after these afflictions, which last but for a moment, whereby He trieth our faith, as gold by the fire, we may everlastingly reign and triumph with Him in the glory of the Father, and that through the same our Lord and Saviour Jesus Christ, to whom with the Father and the Holy Ghost, be all honour and glory, now and for ever, Amen. Amen."

(2) My second extract shall be taken from Ridley's Injunctions to the Diocese of London, given in the year 1550. (Parker Society's edition, p. 319):

"It is injoined, that no minister do counterfeit the Popish Mass in kissing the Lord's board; washing his hands or fingers after the Gospel, or the receipt of the holy Communion; shifting the book from one place to another; laying down and licking the chalice after the Communion; blessing his eyes with the sudarie thereof, or paten, or crossing his head with the same, holding his fore-fingers and thumbs joined together toward the temples of his head, after the receiving of the Sacrament; breathing on the bread, or chalice; saying the Agnus before the Communion; shewing the Sacrament openly before the distribution, or making any elevation thereof; ringing of the sacring bell, or setting any light upon the Lord's board. And finally, that the minister, in the time of the Holy Communion, do use only the ceremonies and gestures appointed by the Book of Common Prayer, and none other, so that there do not appear in them any counterfeiting of the Popish Mass.

"And whereas in divers places some use the Lord's board after the form of a table, and some of an altar, whereby dissension is perceived to arise among the unlearned; therefore, wishing a godly unity to be observed in all our diocese, and for that the form of a table may more move and turn the simple from the old superstitious opinions of the Popish Mass and to the right use of the Lord's Supper, we exhort the curates, churchwardens, and questmen here present, to erect and set up the Lord's board after the form of an honest table decently covered, in such place of the quire or chancel as shall be thought most meet by their discretion and agreement, so that the ministers, with the communicants, may have their place separated from the rest of the people; and to take down and abolish all other by-altars or tables."

(3) My third extract shall be taken from Ridley's letter to Bishop Hooper when they were both in prison, expecting death. It is a remarkable letter, when we remember that the two famous Reformers had once differed much about vestments (Parker Society's edition, p. 355):

"My dearly beloved brother and fellow-elder, whom I reverence in the Lord, pardon me, I beseech you, that hitherto, since your captivity and mine, I have not saluted you by my letters: whereas, I do indeed confess, I have received from you (such was your gentleness) two letters at sundry times, but yet at such times as I could not be suffered to write unto you again; or if I might have written, yet was I greatly in doubt, lest my letters should not safely come unto your hands. But now, my dear brother, forasmuch as I understand by your works, which I have yet but superficially seen, that we thoroughly agree and wholly consent together in those things which are the grounds and substantial points of our religion, against the which the world so furiously rageth in these our days, howsoever in time past in smaller matters and circumstances of religion, your wisdom and my simplicity (I confess) have in some points varied: now, I say, be you assured, that even with my whole heart (God is my witness) in the bowels of Christ, I love you, and in truth; for the truth's sake which abideth in us, and (as I am persuaded) shall by the grace of God abide with us for evermore. And because the world, as I perceive, brother, ceaseth not to play his pageant, and busily conspireth against Christ our Saviour with all possible force and power, exalting high things against the knowledge of God, let us join hands together in Christ; and if we cannot overthrow, yet to our power, and as much as in us lieth, let us shake those things, not with carnal, but with spiritual weapons; and withal, brother, let us prepare ourselves to the day of our dissolution; whereby, after the short time of this bodily affliction, by the grace of our Lord Jesus Christ, we shall triumph together with Him in eternal glory."

(4) My last extract shall be taken from Ridley's farewell letter to the prisoners in Christ's cause. (Parker Society's edition, p. 425):

"Why should we Christians fear death? Can death deprive us of Christ, which is all our comfort, our joy, and our life? Nay, forsooth. But contrary, death shall deliver us from this mortal body, which loadeth and beareth down the spirit, that it cannot so well perceive heavenly things, in the which so long as we dwell, we are absent from God.

"Wherefore, understanding our state in that we be Christians, that if our mortal body, which is our earthly house, were destroyed, we have a building, a house not made with hands, but everlasting in heaven, etc.; therefore we are of good cheer, and know that when we are in the body, we are absent from God; for we walk by faith, and not by clear sight. Nevertheless we are bold, and had rather be absent from the body and present with God. Wherefore we strive, whether we be present at home or absent abroad, that we may always please Him.

"And who that hath true faith in our Saviour Christ, whereby he knoweth somewhat truly what Christ our Saviour is, that He is the eternal Son of God, life, light, the wisdom of the Father, all goodness, all righteousness, and whatsoever is good that heart can desire, yea, infinite plenty of all these, above that that man's heart can either conceive or think (for in Him dwelleth the fulness of the Godhead corporally), and also that He is given us of the Father, 'and made of God to be our wisdom, our righteousness, our holiness, and our redemption;' who (I say) is he that believeth this indeed, that would not gladly be with his Master Christ? Paul for this knowledge coveted to have been loosed from the body, and to have been with Christ, for that he counted it much better for himself, and had rather to be loosed than to live. Therefore these words of Christ to the thief on the cross, that asked of Him mercy, were full of comfort and solace: 'This day thou shalt be with Me in paradise'. To die in the defence of Christ's Gospel, it is our bounden duty to Christ, and also to our neighbour. To Christ, 'for He died for us, and rose again, that He might be Lord over all.' And seeing He died for us, 'we also (saith St John) should jeopard, yea give, our life for our brethren.' And this kind of giving and losing is getting and winning indeed; for he that giveth or loseth his life thus, getteth and winneth it for evermore. 'Blessed are they, therefore, that die in the Lord;' and if they die in the Lord's cause, they are most happy of all.

"Let us not then fear death, which can do us no harm, otherwise than for a moment to make the flesh to smart; for that our faith, which is surely fastened and fixed unto the Word of God, telleth us that we shall be anon after death in peace, in the hands of God, in joy, in solace, and that from death we shall go straight unto life. For St John saith, 'He that liveth and believeth in Me shall never die.' And in another place, 'He shall depart from death unto life.' And therefore this death of the Christian is not to be called death, but rather a gate or entrance into everlasting life. Therefore Paul calleth it but a dissolution and resolution, and both Peter and Paul, a putting off of this tabernacle or dwell-house, meaning thereby the mortal body, as wherein the soul or spirit doth dwell here in this world for a small time. Yea, this death may be called, to the Christian, an end of all miseries. For so long as we live here, 'we must pass through many tribulations, before we can enter into the kingdom of heaven.' And now, after that death has shot his bolt, all the Christian man's enemies have done what they can, and after that they have no more to do. What could hurt or harm poor 'Lazarus, that lay at the rich man's gate'? his former penury and poverty, his miserable beggary, and horrible sores and sickness? For so soon as death had stricken him with his dart, so soon came the angels and carried him straight up into Abraham's bosom. What lost he by death, who from misery and pain is set by the ministry of angels in a place both of joy and solace?

"Farewell, dear brethren, farewell! and let us comfort our hearts in all troubles, and in death, with the Word of God: for heaven and earth shall perish, but the Word of the Lord endureth for ever."

SOME OTHER
BANNER OF TRUTH
TITLES

CHRISTIAN LEADERS OF THE 18th CENTURY

J. C. Ryle

Although much has been written on the evangelical revival of the 18th century, J. C. Ryle's account remains the best popular introduction to this great spiritual era. With simplicity and vigour, he traces the lives of the eleven Christian leaders who 'shook England from one end to another', giving strong reasons for his belief 'that excepting Luther and his Continental contemporaries, and our own martyred Reformers, the world has seen no such men since the days of the apostles.'

But Ryle does not write to prompt admiration, and his conclusions and applications of his subject are among the most forceful that ever came from his pen. 'I am obliged to say plainly that, in my judgment, we have among us neither the men nor the doctrines of the days gone by . . . Once let the evangelical ministry return to the ways of the 18th century, and I firmly believe we should have as much success as before. We are where we are, because we have come short of our fathers.'

At the beginning of this century, Canon A. M. W. Christopher of St Aldate's, Oxford, declared that he had turned to Ryle's book during every summer vacation for thirty years. It is time *Christian Leaders* was so read again.

ISBN 0 85151 268 2
432pp. Paperback

EXPOSITORY THOUGHTS ON THE GOSPELS

J. C. Ryle

Ryle's chief aim is to help the reader to know Christ. He also has another object in view. He writes so that his commentaries can be read aloud to a group. There are many other fuller commentaries on the Gospels, but no others make such compelling listening—whether it be in the family, in neighbourhood groups, or over the air—as those of J. C. Ryle.

Matthew ISBN 0 85151 483 9
408pp. Paperback

Mark ISBN 0 85151 441 3
384pp. Paperback

Luke: Volume 1 ISBN 0 85151 497 9
416pp. Paperback

Luke: Volume 2 ISBN 0 85151 498 7
560pp. Paperback

John: Volume 1 ISBN 0 85151 504 5
448pp. Paperback

John: Volume 2 ISBN 0 85151 505 3
448pp. Paperback

John: Volume 3 ISBN 0 85151 506 1
552pp. Paperback

For further details and a free illustrated catalogue please write to:
THE BANNER OF TRUTH TRUST
3 Murrayfield Road, Edinburgh EH12 6EL
P.O. Box 621, Carlisle, Pennsylvania, 17013, U.S.A.